PASSING TH...

Guide Your Child to Fo... ...s

Group

Loveland, Colorado
group.com

Group resources actually work!

This Group resource incorporates our R.E.A.L. approach to ministry. It reinforces a growing friendship with Jesus, encourages long-term learning, and results in life transformation, because it's

Relational
Learner-to-learner interaction enhances learning and builds Christian friendships.

Experiential
What learners experience through discussion and action sticks with them up to 9 times longer than what they simply hear or read.

Applicable
The aim of Christian education is to equip learners to be both hearers and doers of God's Word.

Learner-based
Learners understand and retain more when the learning process takes into consideration how they learn best.

Passing the Baton
Guide Your Child to Follow Jesus

Visit our website: **group.com**

Credits
Senior Editor: Candace McMahan
Creative Development Editor: Patty Smith
Chief Creative Officer: Joani Schultz
Copy Editor: Lyndsay Gerwing
Art Director: Jeff A. Storm
Print Production Artist: Greg Longbons
Cover Photographer: Craig DeMartino
Production Manager: DeAnne Lear

Unless otherwise indicated, all Scripture quotations are taken from the *Holy Bible* New Living Translation, copyright © 1996, 2004, 2007. Used by permission of Tyndale House Publishers, Carol Stream, Illinois 60188. All rights reserved.

Library of Congress Cataloging-in-Publication Data
Edwards, Grant, 1947-
  Passing the baton : guide your child to follow Jesus / Grant Edwards.
-- 1st American pbk. ed.
      p. cm.
  ISBN 978-0-7644-3875-2 (pbk. : alk. paper)
 1. Christian education--Home training. 2. Christian education of children.
 3. Children--Religious life. I. Title.
  BV1590.E34 2009
  248.8'45--dc22
                                    2009002490

  10 9 8 7 6 5 4 3 2 1   18 17 16 15 14 13 12 11 10 09

Printed in the United States of America.

Contents

Introduction

Everything you need to know to launch an amazing, life-changing discipling relationship with your child.

New parents discover pretty quickly how many people it takes to raise a child.

There's a pediatrician, of course, plus enough nurses to staff a moderate-sized hospital. Along with teeth comes a dentist, and within a few years there's a regular parade of preschool and school teachers in the mix. Add coaches, swim instructors, band directors, camp counselors, Sunday school teachers, and scout masters, and soon you're way past that village you were told it would take to raise your little one.

Somehow, you've engaged an entire *city* in the project.

But one piece of the puzzle belongs to you—and you alone. It's ultimately *your* responsibility to disciple your children. The fact that you're reading this book is an indication that you've embraced that responsibility. Good for you.

Because, in reality, you're *already* discipling your child.

Do as I Say...*and* as I Do

Studies confirm the obvious: Parents are the primary faith-shapers in the lives of their children. The biggest influence in your child's spiritual development isn't a Sunday school teacher or pastor. It's not the religion teacher at school.

It's you.

For better or worse, children learn how to live by watching their parents. Kids soak up our attitudes, watch our example.

Scary thought, huh? You know how often your child has seen you at your worst.

But consider these words from Deuteronomy 6:6-7:

> *"These commandments that I give you today are to be upon your hearts. Impress them on your children. Talk about them when you sit at home and when you walk along the road, when you lie down and when you get up"* (New International Version).

God *intended* for you to provide the chief spiritual example for your child. And the place of greatest impact isn't a special occasion or church retreat—it's daily life.

You're the person best able to give your child the heart and skills to engage Jesus in a lifelong friendship. God has placed you in a spot of enormous influence, has given you a tender heart toward your child, and provides the power of his Holy Spirit to enable you to raise your child up to know, love, and honor him.

And knowing all that—you're probably terrified.

There's little as daunting as the thought of discipling your own child…for two reasons.

1. Your Child Knows You…the Real You

Your child knows you don't pray as often as you should, that you can go a week without cracking your Bible. Isn't it hypocritical to encourage your child to grow in areas where you, too, could use improvement?

Nope…because you'll *never* be a perfect example for your child to follow. There will *always* be areas in your life in which you need to grow.

Use the next 10 weeks to let God deepen *your* life in him, too. If you've failed to honor God in some way, let your child see and hear you repent, be forgiven, and move on in faithfulness.

It's a powerful example.

2. You're Not Quite Sure What to Do

Relax, we've got you covered.

Discipling is the process of teaching young Christians those things they need to know to be established in their faith. It's helping someone fall in love with Jesus.

And it's easier than you think.

Young Christians—like your child—need to know just a few key things to grow in their relationships with Jesus. They're the same things necessary to grow in *any* relationship, so most of what you'll do is help your child form habits and patterns that make for growing friendships.

The principles in this book are biblical, practical, and proven. They've set young believers on the course of lifelong spiritual growth thousands of times, in churches around the world.

And we'll walk you through the process step by step.

So take a deep breath and get ready for an adventure—one you'll share with your child. One that draws your child deeper into a loving relationship with God. One that sets your child on a path that will change his or her life for eternity.

First, Some Practical Stuff

Before you dive into the first session, nail down these details:

Get the Right Bibles

Give your child a Bible appropriate for his or her reading level.

Consider using the *Hands-On Bible* (Group Publishing, Inc. and Tyndale House Publishers, 2004). It uses the New Living Translation—a clear, simple version that engages children and makes the meaning of passages clear.

The New Living Translation is written at a sixth-grade reading level—though younger readers usually have no problem reading the text.

No matter what version you select, pick up a copy for yourself, too. That way you and your child will be on the same page—literally!

Plan Week 10

In week 10 you'll treat your child to a special time with you. You'll decide what that is, but expect it to cost a few dollars. Plan now so your budget can absorb the extra cost.

You'll also pray a blessing over your child in week 10. To help you prepare a meaningful blessing, we've provided a "Blessed to Be a Blessing" section each week. In each are several questions that help you sort out who your child is and how God may be directing your child.

Your influence in guiding your child can't be overemphasized. The blessing you'll pray mirrors a practice seen often in the Old Testament—and it will have a huge impact on your child.

So it's important you "study" your child throughout this discipling process. Ask God how to speak into your child's life, how God's wired your child for service in the kingdom, how you can best cooperate with God's purposes for your child.

Schedule 45 Minutes per Week

Put time for discipling in your schedule, your child's schedule, on the family schedule—everywhere. Treat this time as untouchable.

Kids are accustomed to being shuffled around for their parents' convenience. When you treat this appointment as important, that sends a message: Discipling is important, too.

Show up for your discipling times refreshed, relaxed, and unhurried. Discipling your child isn't something to cram in as you're dashing off to something more important; it *is* what's more important.

Do Your Homework

Several times your child will be asked to learn a memory verse or do some reading. Do the same—and *not* at the last minute. If possible, arrange for your child to *see* you doing the prep work.

And while we've suggested what you might say during sessions, don't use this book as a script. Put the principles and points in your own words. Pull from experiences in your own life, and the life of your child, for examples.

Determine What Sort of Child You're Discipling

Take a look at the temperament styles on pages 10-11. We've described three general personality categories, and odds are good one of them most closely resembles your child.

Each week we'll suggest activities designed to appeal to each of these personalities. Why? Because children don't all learn the same way—and you want your child to embrace discipling naturally and deeply. It makes sense to tailor the material to your child.

Feel free to use any or all of the activities; they all make the same point and cover the same material. It's your choice!

If Your Child Wants to Do More, We've Got You Covered

You'll find an "Extras!" section after each week's session. You can watch a movie with your child, take a hike through your neighborhood, join your child in doing a quick art project, or even play a game. All the extras reinforce what you discovered together in the week's session.

Show your child the "Extras!" section each week, and let your child choose one or more of the activities to pursue. Even better: Make photocopies of those pages, and give them to your child. You have our permission!

Turn This Book Into a Memory-Making Scrapbook

You'll find a scrapbook page at the end of each session. Completing it creates a snapshot in time of these days, and when your child leafs through this book in years to come, it will help him or her remember this time with you and with Jesus.

As you work on these pages, you'll focus on your child. Use the time to pray for—and thank God for—the honor of parenting your child.

Pray—a Lot

What you're doing has eternal consequences. Pray daily for wisdom and patience, for faithfulness, for your child and yourself. Ask others to pray specifically for you, and update your prayer requests as you move through these sessions.

Batons and Prayer Pages

If you're doing this discipling process as part of a church program, you probably received a baton—a metal or plastic baton used in track and field relay races—at your launch party. If you don't have a baton, they're easy enough to find at a sporting goods store or by looking up "sports batons" on the Internet.

Before your first session, make several copies of page 144 so you'll have Prayer Pages to roll up and tuck into the baton. Throughout the discipling sessions, you'll be encouraged to pull out those pages and write down what you're praying for your child.

Please don't skip this step. Those pages will be passed along to your child at the end of this program and will be a precious reminder of your faithfulness in prayer, of your love, and of what you've asked God to do in and through your child.

Plus, what you pray will help you formulate a blessing for your child—more about that in session 10.

Keep the baton where your child can see it as you go through these sessions. It's a reminder of the journey you're taking together.

If you're part of a group, you'll give your baton to your child at the closing celebration. If you're not part of a group, see page 126 of session 10, "Pass the Baton."

Sign the Covenant

You'll find a Covenant—an agreement you and your child sign together—on page 137. If you're part of a church program, you'll sign a Covenant at the launch party. But if you're working through this discipling process on your own, make a copy of the Covenant and go through it with your child.

This will set expectations, build excitement, and bond you and your child together in this adventure of discipleship.

Once you've signed the Covenant, slip it into the baton. In time you'll pass it along to your child.

If You're Part of a Group...

If your pastor or children's pastor has recruited a group of parents to disciple their children at the same time (a good idea!), be sure you attend the group's launch party. And go to the closing celebration, too.

See Chapters 11 and 12 for detailed information about the opening and closing celebrations.

SPOILER ALERT: Don't read those chapters unless you're leading the events—it's more fun to be surprised!

How to Personalize These Discipling Sessions

God's wired each child to be unique—and that's a good thing! The world would be a poorer place if every child had the same strengths and weaknesses and liked the same flavor of ice cream.

Some kids are naturally energetic and others patient. Some enjoy details while others are "big picture" visionaries. Kids come with different temperaments—and different learning styles.

Asked to do a project, Jackie jumps right in, figuring it out as she goes. Bob carefully reads all the directions first. And Sue wants to talk through how to proceed; that's how she processes information best.

Before you begin discipling your child, decide this: What's your child's temperament?

Three Temperament Styles

Your child will learn best if you tailor discipling sessions to fit your child's temperament. After each session you'll find three different application activities—each tailored to a specific temperament.

Look at the categories below and decide which of the three toys best describes your child. It won't be an exact match—God's wired your child to be unique, remember—but you'll see similarities.

There's no right or wrong temperament. And the goal isn't to label your child. Yet, if you have a grade-A, bona fide "Jigsaw Puzzle," you'll find your child learns more if you provide opportunities that play to his strengths. The same is true for the other temperament styles.

Check out the descriptions below:

Jigsaw Puzzles

These children enjoy carefully coloring in every corner of the picture— the *right* way. They're capable of diving into adventure, but they seem happiest when doing detailed, orderly tasks and arranging the parts and pieces just so.

Words that describe Jigsaw Puzzles include:

perfectionist
pragmatic
matter-of-fact
reserved
analytical
thoughtful
careful
calculating

restrained

painstaking

SuperBalls

Yee-hah! These spontaneous, fun-loving kids ricochet from one thing to the next, making friends and connections as they go. Passionate, positive, and seldom pooped, SuperBalls have two speeds: "on" and "asleep."

Words that describe SuperBalls include:

passionate

independent

verbal

friendly

easily bored

ringleader

spontaneous

creative

determined

enthusiastic

Teddy Bears

These sensitive, warm children may seem older than they actually are, their patience and relational abilities tacking a few years onto their chronological age. They can identify the feelings of others and are likely to be voted "most likely to become a diplomat" by their peers.

Words that describe Teddy Bears include:

tenderhearted

hesitant

sympathetic

nonconfrontational

loyal

comfortable with routine

flexible

accepting

nurturing

Tending the Toy Box

Which one of these toys best describes your child? Jot your answer below:

_____

As you move through discipling sessions, take note of the follow-up application activities for each temperament type. It's up to you (and your child) which activities to do, but generally your child will be drawn to activities designed for her temperament.

All the activities reinforce the same Bible truths and spiritual development skills; they're equally effective.

But they'll *only* be effective if your child actually *does* them—so be sure to select activities that match your child's energy level and natural wiring.

And It's Time to Begin

You've scheduled your 10 sessions. You have the right tools in hand. You've dedicated this time to God.

Get ready for some fun!

1

Welcome to the Family

Your child has a special spot in the family of God, and God has an adventure planned for your child. You'll discover what it is as you and your child both decide to trust Jesus.

The Point
Jesus wants your child to be his disciple—and to trust him.

What You'll Need
- $5 bill you don't mind losing
- pair of clean socks
- clean cloth blindfold
- earplugs or earphones attached to an MP3 player or portable CD player
- lollipop (or other hard candy)
- several sturdy chairs
- two Bibles

Welcome to the Family
Adults sometimes think of children as "associate" Christians, too young to do *real* ministry. Too young to have a *real* faith.

And nothing could be further from the truth.

Jesus doesn't discriminate on the basis of age. When people enter into a relationship with him, he meets them where they are—even if they're in elementary school.

Your child can have a relationship with Jesus. But if it's not nurtured, it will do what any neglected relationship does: wither away.

You won't teach your child theology or nail down doctrine during the next 10 weeks. But you will *encourage a loving relationship with Jesus.* The rest of what your child needs to know—how to navigate the Bible, what an offering plate is for, the finer points of church potlucks—will come later.

Keep your focus on your child's *relationship with Jesus.* It's what will prompt faithful living and lifelong discipleship.

Nothing is more important than that growing friendship with Jesus.

In this session you'll help your child discover that a relationship with Jesus grows deeper if we do several simple things:

- pray,
- read the Bible,
- fellowship, and
- share our faith story.

The rest of the discipling sessions will help you integrate these disciplines into the life of your child… as well as your own.

Dive In

Find the Fiver (15 minutes)

Say: I have a $5 bill for you. It's a gift; there are no strings attached. I'll place it in plain sight, and all you have to do is pick it up. Sound easy enough?

Of course, this assumes that you can do a few things.

You'll need to see the bill, which is hard to do when you're wearing a blindfold. (Tie the blindfold over your child's eyes.)

And you have to pick it up, which is tough when you're wearing sock mittens. (Pull the socks onto your child's hands.)

I think you can *taste* money, too, so I'll put a lollipop in your mouth. (Give your child the candy.)

And just in case the bill calls out to you, I'll put these earphones on you…playing music *I* like! Once you hear the music, wait 10 seconds and then go get the bill. Ready?

Place the earphones in your child's ears, place the bill somewhere in the room, and then wait 45 seconds before removing the earphones.

Say: So far it's not going very well. Maybe if you give up the lollipop. Take the lollipop and wait 45 seconds.

Say: Still not working. Tell you what: I'll take off the socks. Do so and wait 45 seconds as your child searches.

Say: OK, off with the blindfold! Your child will quickly locate the bill.

Say: The gift is yours to keep. I wanted you to have this good gift, but it took you awhile to claim it.

Ask your child the following questions, and discuss your child's answers:

• What made finding this gift difficult?

• What made getting this gift easier?

Say: It was hard to receive this gift when you were distracted and other things got in the way. The gift was there, waiting for you, but you had to pursue it and not let other things get in your way.

A growing friendship with Jesus is like that, too. Jesus loves you and wants a close, growing friendship with you. There are gifts he wants to give you, too:

He wants to give you an exciting life full of adventure.

He wants you to have joy.

He wants you to be with him forever in heaven.

But no gift is more precious than his love and the chance to follow him as his disciple.

In the next few weeks we'll talk about how to be Jesus' disciple, how to follow him, how to know and trust him, and how to grow in your friendship with him.

And it's gonna be an adventure!

Dig In

Why Trust Jesus? (20 minutes)

Ask your child to stand on a sturdy chair as you read "Leap of Faith Story 1" (p. 19).

At the end of the story, ask your child to jump to the floor.

Discuss these questions with your child:

• How would it feel to leap into the darkness?

• What helped the friends take the leap?

Say: We were like those friends. We were stuck in sin with no way out. And the Bible says the price we pay for sinning is death!

Read Romans 3:23 and Romans 6:23 aloud. If your child is able, ask your child to read the passages.

Say: If you've taken the leap of trusting Jesus to be your friend, that's great—and he wants to *be* your friend! But there's another leap we need to take, too—a next step. You also have to trust Jesus enough to be his *disciple*, to serve him.

A disciple is someone who follows Jesus daily. It's not a one-time thing; it's every day, day after day. It's loving Jesus enough to go where he sends you, to do what he wants you to do.

We can be disciples...but to follow Jesus, we first have to trust him.

Let's look at four reasons we can trust Jesus.

Reason 1: Jesus Knows You

Read Luke 12:6-8.

Say: Do you know how many hairs you have on your head? Take a guess. The number depends on your hair color and age, but it's probably around 100,000. And you lose between 50 and 100 hairs every day.

Jesus knows *exactly* how many you have. He knows your name. He knows everything about you—your needs, your wants, who your friends are, and what you're afraid of.

It's easier to trust someone when that person knows you...and you get to know that person.

• Who's someone you didn't trust at first but came to trust as you got to know each other?

Reason 2: Jesus Loves You

Read John 3:16 and Romans 5:8 together.

Say: Jesus loves you with his whole heart—so much that he died in your place so you could be forgiven for the wrong things you've done.

Ask: • How does it feel to know Jesus loves you that much?

Reason 3: Jesus Wants What's Best for You

Read John 10:10 and Romans 8:28 together.

Say: Jesus will never trick you or make fun of you. He will never hurt you. He wants you to grow into a person who honors God and stands for the truth. That's a friend who helps you become all you can be!

Ask: • What's something Jesus has asked you to do?

DISCIPLER TIP

Make sure all your questions are open-ended, that is, they can't be answered with a simple "yes" or "no." They should draw out what your child really thinks and feels. Follow up answers your child gives you with additional questions, digging deeper, but always make the questions open-ended. They keep the good stuff coming!

Reason 4: Jesus Wants to Be Your Friend—Forever

Read John 14:3 together.

Say: Most friendships come and go. Think about your friends a few years ago. Have you added any friends since then?

Pause to identify friendships that have lasted and faded.

Say: Jesus wants to be your forever friend—to be a friend today, tomorrow, and always. For that to happen, we have to keep growing in our friendship with him. The way to do that is to become a disciple—to know, love, and follow Jesus.

- What's something you know or love about Jesus?

Ask your child to climb back on a sturdy chair. Get on a sturdy chair or step stool yourself, and read aloud "Leap of Faith Story 2" (p. 20).

At the end of the story, invite your child to jump to the floor with you.

Say: In the next 10 weeks, we'll have fun learning simple ways to know, love, and follow Jesus. That's the adventure Jesus has for you: a lifetime of following him.

So let's get to know him better together!

Make It Mine

Shhhhh! (10 minutes)

Say: This week let's jump into the adventure of trusting Jesus.

In Matthew 6:1-4 Jesus tells us to give to others without expecting anything in return. Jesus says God will see what we do and reward us. So this week let's give to the needy without getting any credit for it.

- Who do we know who needs something? What does the person need? How might we help?

It's important that your child can actually see the person you select to help. This won't be a memorable experience if you simply send a check to a distant mission organization.

Choose a project from the "Operation: Trust Jesus" section (pp. 18-19) that fits your child. Or, even better, work to accomplish a project selected by your child.

> "Trust in the Lord with all your heart; do not depend on your own understanding. Seek his will in all you do; and he will show you which path to take."
> —*Proverbs 3:5-6*

Blessed to Be a Blessing

Extending trust is difficult for some people, including children. Even the people who met Jesus face to face during his earthly ministry didn't all choose to trust him.

The most convincing argument that Jesus is trustworthy is…you. Your life. If your child sees that you trust Jesus and obey him, that says it all to your child.

So this week, be intentional about modeling discipleship. When you tell stories about your day, include those moments that you did the right thing, not because it was easy but because that's what Jesus did.

Demonstrate *your* trust in Jesus, and you'll see that trust reflected in your child's life.

- In what ways do you demonstrate trust in Jesus?
- How trusting is your child by nature? Why do you answer as you do?
- In what practical ways can you encourage your child's trust in Jesus this week?

> "Trust everybody, but cut the cards."
> —*Finley Peter Dunne*

Pray

Dear God, you know the power of trust, of faith, of taking you at your word. Give my child a deep, solid trust in you and Jesus. Show me how to help that trust take root and grow throughout my child's life. Amen.

Operation: Trust Jesus

Objective: To give something meaningful to someone in need—without getting credit for the gift.

Jigsaw Puzzles

Ask your child to design a card by hand or on a computer and to then anonymously deliver the card to someone who needs encouragement.

If your child is musical, consider how to write and/or play a song or piece of music for others—without being identified as the musician.

SuperBalls

Encourage your child to organize a group effort to meet a need.

Here are some ideas:

- a neighborhood food drive with the proceeds going to a specific family in need identified through your church,
- a community effort to clean up the property of an elderly or bedridden person, or
- launching a prayer chain to support someone in need.

Teddy Bears

Work with your child to write an encouraging, uplifting note and get the note into the hands of a discouraged person—without the person knowing who wrote the note.

The note could be slipped into a locker or coat pocket, sent through the mail anonymously, left under a windshield wiper, or taped to a bouquet of flowers and placed where it's sure to be found.

Leap of Faith Story 1

Two friends were hiking in the mountains. The day had been perfect—sunny and warm. But late in the afternoon, the sky suddenly grew dark. The friends saw storm clouds rushing toward them. The temperature dropped. Snow and sleet slashed at their thin clothes.

The friends were stuck on a rock ledge. It was dark, and the friends were freezing. They had just enough power in a cell phone to make one call to 911.

The 911 operator couldn't help but patched them through to a man who said, "I know right where you are. About 10 feet below you is another ledge. If you jump, you'll land on it and find a cave. There's shelter from the storm, and in the morning we'll come get you."

The two friends couldn't see a ledge beneath them. It was too dark. Jump off the mountain and maybe fall hundreds of feet to their deaths? That was asking a lot!

As their cell phone reception faded, they asked who they were talking to. It was a forest ranger and expert mountain climber who'd worked in the mountains for years.

So they jumped—and found the ledge.
They lived through the night.

Leap of Faith Story 2

Two friends were living in [name of your city]. Most of their days were great, but sometimes they ran into hard times. Times that school or work didn't go well. Times they were angry or sad.

Sometimes they felt they knew exactly what to do. Other times they didn't have a clue.

Every day there was a voice that called out to them. The voice said, "Trust me. I know you, so trust me. I love you, so trust me. I want what's best for you, so trust me. I want to be your friend forever, so trust me."

The friends heard the voice every morning, and every morning they had to decide if they would trust the voice. If they would listen and obey.

They knew who was speaking. It was Jesus.

So the friends had to decide: Were they willing to take the leap?

EXTRAS!

FILM FUN!

Fire up the microwave popcorn—it's time for a movie!

But before you settle down in front of the TV, have a parent check out the film we've suggested. Families have different standards when it comes to movies. Your parent will decide if this movie is appropriate entertainment.

Have the remote control in hand? the popcorn buttered? Enjoy!

Film: *Finding Nemo* (rated G)
Length: 1 hour, 40 minutes

Plot

Marlin may be a clown fish, but he's not laughing. After losing his wife in an attack, he's scared to let his son, Nemo, go out into open water. *Ever.* Even to get to *school.*

And sure enough, when Nemo defies his father and swims away to check out a boat, he's scooped up by a diver. Nemo ends up in an aquarium in a dentist's office.

But Marlin isn't giving up! He's going to find his son…no matter what it takes.

The Connection

God is on a mission! He wants to bring you, your friends, and anyone who wants to join you into his family. And God has done a *lot* to have people get to know him.

God walked in the Garden of Eden with Adam and Eve. He then gave us the Ten Commandments to help us know him. He shared his words to and through his prophets. He sent his Son, Jesus, to show us what God's like. He inspired people to write the Bible. And he sent the Holy Spirit to live in us.

God has done everything he could to make it clear: We're welcome in his family!

While you and your parent watch this movie, think about how Marlin wouldn't give up searching for his child. And think about how God hasn't given up searching for his children—including you and your parent!

After the Film

Talk with a parent about these questions:
- What would it be like to have Marlin for a dad?
- How does Marlin show his love to Nemo?
- What's it like to have God for a heavenly Father?
- How does God show his love to us?

 **GAME FUN!**

Greetings!

You're welcome in God's family! How do you think God will greet you when you get to heaven? With a handshake? a hug? a kiss on both cheeks? There are lots of ways to say hello!

Check out the chart on page 23. See if you can match up the country on the left with the custom for saying hello on the right. When you've finished, check your answers.

But don't do this alone—invite a parent to join you. Let's see who knows more about making people around the world feel welcome. And ask your parent how he or she thinks God says hello.

And no cheating! Don't look at the answers before you try to match up the countries and customs.

1. China	A. Firm, solid handshake
2. Germany	B. When greeting male friends, men kiss each other on one or both cheeks.
3. Mozambique	C. Place both hands together in front of the chest and bow.
4. France	D. Hug while exchanging breaths
5. England	E. Press noses together
6. Cambodia	F. Press fists together
7. Italy	G. A low bow, with eyes lowered
8. Texas	H. A gentle handshake, followed by a kiss on both cheeks
9. Native Hawaiians	I. Men seldom face each other directly; they stand at a slight angle.
10. Belize	J. Brief, firm handshake
11. New Zealand	K. Place open palms together, like a light handclap.

Check your answers here.

1 = G; 2 = A; 3 = K; 4 = H; 5 = I; 6 = C; 7 = B; 8 = J; 9 = D; 10 = F; 11 = E

Make up a special handshake or greeting, and use it this week to greet your friends!

ART START!

Looks like you're being welcomed to the family with a party! Draw your favorite party treats on the platter. And draw enough to share!

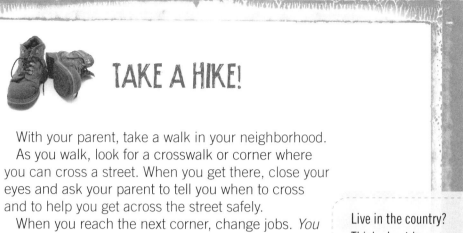

TAKE A HIKE!

With your parent, take a walk in your neighborhood.

As you walk, look for a crosswalk or corner where you can cross a street. When you get there, close your eyes and ask your parent to tell you when to cross and to help you get across the street safely.

When you reach the next corner, change jobs. *You* be the guide who helps your parent cross the street safely.

As you complete your brief hike, talk about these questions:

- What makes it scary to trust others?
- In what ways do you trust Jesus? In what ways could you trust Jesus more?

Live in the country? Think about how you can do this hike where *you* live.

SCRAPBOOK MEMORY MAKER!

Family Table

Draw the family table. Who sits at it (or under it—remember Fido!)? What about extended family? friends as close as family?

If there are two or more tables in different homes, draw them all.

Friends Forever

Good news: Jesus wants to be your child's friend—now and forever. Your child will get to know Jesus and discover what sort of friendship he wants to have with your child.

The Point
Disciples have a loving friendship with Jesus—and that love prompts obedience.

What You'll Need
- paper and pencils
- two Bibles
- two key blanks from the hardware store (Buy just the blanks; don't have the keys ground so they open something.)
- key from your key chain that's been ground to open a car or door

Obedience for All the Right Reasons
Think of a time when your child was small that she disobeyed a rule and headed straight toward disaster. Maybe she was drifting into dangerously deep water at a neighbor's pool, chasing a ball that had bounced into the street, or slipping out of a seat belt to reach for a dropped piece of candy.

You called out in a voice that froze your child in her tracks, and a tragedy was averted. That part's good: You kept your child safe.

But it's even *better* when our children choose to obey us when we *aren't* around to shout out warnings—when our children obey not out of fear that we'll catch them doing something wrong but because they love us and want to please us.

Obedience motivated by fear works only when we're lurking in the background, ready to pounce. But obedience motivated by love holds firm when your child is out of your sight. It holds firm when others are cheating or compromising, when others bully or lie.

God wants us to obey him, but out of love—to be drawn to his character out of love, not fear. That's the relationship he wants with us because that's the relationship he offers us: that of a loving father who expects obedience—but obedience for all the right reasons.

Dive In

Do as I Say (15 minutes)

Say: It's hard to take adults seriously sometimes, isn't it?

Adults don't always do what they ask *you* to do, like taking out the trash, cleaning their rooms, or obeying. You have to obey a lot of people. Who are all the people you obey?

Allow time for your child's response.

Say: I'm an adult. Who do you think *I* have to obey?

Allow time for your child's response.

Say: I obey my boss at work. I obey the people I love when they ask me to do things, as long as they're good things to do. But most important, I obey Jesus.

Obeying Jesus is especially tough because he asks me to do things like be kind to people who aren't kind to me and care for people I don't even know.

But here's a great reason to take Jesus seriously: He did everything he asks us to do—even the tough stuff.

He loved people even when they were mean to him.

He was patient with his friends even when he had to repeat himself again and again.

He felt pain—more pain than I've ever felt—when he hung on the cross.

He even died, like we'll both do one day.

And he did all these things out of obedience to God, his Father.

Have your child look up and read aloud John 14:23-24.

Discuss the following questions:
- Do you always obey people because you love them? Why else might you obey someone?
- Which do you think is most important: loving Jesus or obeying him? Why?
- Why do you think Jesus asks people who love him to do what he says?

Say: Jesus wants us to obey him, but not just because he's so powerful. He wants us to obey because we love him, because we trust that he loves us and wants what's best for us.

Disciples are followers of Jesus, and that means we need to obey Jesus. But not because we're afraid. Instead, he wants us to obey out of love!

Dig In

House Rules (10 minutes)

Say: According to lots of Internet sites, it's against the law in Massachusetts to have a duel with water pistols and in New York City for citizens to say hello to each other by putting their thumbs to their noses and wiggling their fingers. But even though those laws may be written down, people aren't often arrested for breaking them. There are rules, and then there are *rules*—really important rules that count!

Give your child a pencil and a sheet of notebook paper. Keep a pencil and sheet of paper yourself.

Say: I want you to think of the seven biggest, most important rules in our house—the rules that get you in real trouble if you break them. Write them down on your paper.

I'm going to write down the seven rules I think are most important in our house. Then we'll compare our lists and see if they're the same. And no cheating—I won't look at your paper, and you can't look at mine.

Ready? Let's take three minutes to write down the rules.

After three minutes, put down your pencil, and ask your child to do the same. If your child couldn't come up with seven rules, that's fine—work with what you have.

Say: Let's compare lists.

Switch lists and see how many rules are the same on your lists.

Ask your child to explain why he selected the rules he listed. Ask if he believes each rule is a good or bad one, and why. What makes it a good or bad rule?

Your child may have
made a commitment
to Jesus without
realizing there's a
do-what-Jesus-says
Lordship element
to the relationship.
Passing the Baton will
begin to bring that
part of the relationship
into focus.
And this program
is also a great time
to confirm that your
child has made a
commitment to Jesus.
Explore that—ask your
child.

"There is no shame
in taking orders from
those who themselves
have learned to obey."
—*William Edward
Forster*

Do the same with your list.
When you've finished, lay down the lists.

Say: I don't want you to obey the rules in our home
because I can punish you if you don't obey. I'd rather you obey
rules because you love me, because you trust that I want what's
best for you.

When we obey only because we're afraid of punishment, as
soon as the person who can punish us is gone, we quit obeying.

I want you to obey me because you love me. Jesus wants you
to obey him for the same reason.

Make It Mine

Love to Obey (5 minutes)

Say: Here's what's tricky about obeying because of love: It
looks just like obeying because you're afraid of being punished.
Like lots of discipleship stuff, this is a matter of the heart.

This week let's work on heart stuff. That's why this week I want
us both to carry these key blanks.

Show your child a key that's been ground to open a
lock. Ask your child to compare the key blanks and the
ground key.

Say: Your key blank won't open any locks because it hasn't
been fitted to the tumblers inside a lock. For it to work on our
house or a car, it has to be shaped a certain way.

Your key looks like it should work, but it won't. Sometimes we
look like we're obeying for the right reason, but we aren't.

This week when you need to obey someone and when I need to
obey someone, let's put our hands in our pockets to feel our key
blanks. The key blanks will remind us that we can choose to obey
for the right reasons—like loving or honoring the person asking
us to obey.

And as we practice obeying for the right reasons, God will
shape our hearts to open to him.

Discuss these questions with your child:

- Are you naturally obedient, disobedient, or somewhere in
between? Why do you answer as you do?
- What will be hardest about obeying this week? Why?

Choose a project from the "For All the Right Reasons"
section (pp. 31-32) that fits your child. Or, even better,
work to accomplish a project selected by your child.

Blessed to Be a Blessing

Do you think that just because you're the grown-up you're off the hook with obedience? Far from it.

Adults struggle with obeying God, too. Every disciple deals with a desire to simply forget what God wants us to do and do our own thing, on our own timetable.

Take seriously your role as a disciple and discipler this week. Carry your key blank, and let it remind you that while you can obey for many reasons, only one lets God do the work he wants to do in us.

And pray for your child, whether your child thought herself disobedient, obedient, or in between.

- What does your child's answer say about her self-image?
- How can you help her celebrate the times she's obedient?

Pray

Dear God, it's strange to think of how you came to earth and had to decide to obey, just as we do. You obeyed your Father out of love, not obligation. Help us obey in the same way, fueled by the same motive. Amen.

For All the Right Reasons

Objective: To practice obedience with people in order to be better able to obey Jesus.

Jigsaw Puzzles

It's chart time!

Ask your Jigsaw Puzzle to think about what he will be asked to do at your house in the coming week and then to create a chart listing those things. Rather than calling this a chore chart, label it an obedience chart.

The goal is for your Jigsaw Puzzle to own this process and see it as practice for obeying Jesus. Help your child brainstorm common requests (picking up clothing, cleaning a room, doing dishes, and so on). Avoid the temptation to pile on tasks; rather, encourage your child to list what he recalls.

BATON PRAYERS

In week 10 or 11, you'll share with your child what you've been praying for him or her. Take a few moments to write on a sheet of paper any long-term prayers you have for your child. Maybe it's to marry a believer or to be a faithful follower all his or her life. Whatever those requests are, write them down, and then roll up the page and slip it into your baton.

"One act of obedience is better than one hundred sermons."
—*Dietrich Bonhoeffer*

Then show appreciation by checking off tasks as they're completed—and lavishly heaping praise on your child for obeying.

SuperBalls

Team up with your SuperBall to do a two-hour obedience marathon. Make a joint list of tasks that you've been asked to do, and then pick a two-hour session in which you attempt to accomplish as many of them as possible together.

Generate a list of small, ongoing tasks. Painting a room is probably out, but you might include cleaning, yardwork, or running errands.

After the two-hour obedience marathon, sit down with a treat and talk about how it felt to obey by choice. Discuss how otherwise boring tasks can be fun when you're anticipating how pleased the person who asked you to do them will be.

Teddy Bears

Together, select someone who normally has requests for one or both of you. It may be another parent, a neighbor who needs help, or a teacher. Decide to honor every request this week—and to do your best to obey the person the same way you'd obey Jesus.

This will require ongoing communication (not a bad thing!) and some joint effort. If your child is asked to pick up his room, do it together. If you're asked to take out the trash, do it as a team.

You'll model obedience. You'll have more time with your child. Plus, you'll make someone very happy!

Extras!

Film Fun!

Ready for a movie? Have a parent preview the film before you watch it. Butter up the popcorn, and enjoy the movie!

Film: *Homeward Bound: The Incredible Journey* (rated G)
Length: 84 minutes

Plot

When a family goes on vacation, they leave behind three pets—Chance (a young dog), Sassy (a snob of a cat), and Shadow (an elderly dog).

The pets don't know what happened to their humans, so they set out to find and rescue their family.

Chance and Sassy aren't fond of each other. But as they face dangerous rivers, mountains, and wild animals, their friendship grows.

The pets keep going, even though they know they're in danger. Their love for their human family is so strong that the pets risk their lives to care for their family.

The Connection

Disciples don't always have all the answers. They don't know how to answer some questions on math tests. They lose their backpacks and keys. They forget phone numbers.

But one thing disciples *do* know: Because they love Jesus, they'll follow him anywhere. Even if it's dangerous.

Disciples don't follow Jesus just because it's the right thing to do or because Jesus told them to follow him. They follow Jesus because they love him.

As you become a disciple, you'll learn more about Jesus, but that's not the point. The point is to actually *know* Jesus so your friendship with Jesus will grow.

You're like those three pets—Chance, Sassy, and Shadow. They made mistakes. They argued. They weren't sure what to do next. But they were faithful followers. And that's exactly what Jesus wants from you: to follow him—every day.

As you watch this movie, see how much the pets love their human family. Think about how much you love Jesus.

After the Film

Talk with a parent about these questions:
- How do Chance, Shadow, and Sassy show their love for their human family?
- How do the humans show their love for their pets?
- Describe a time you felt loved. What was it like?
- What's hardest about following Jesus? What's easiest?

GAME FUN!

10 Questions

You and your parent have known each other a long time. But do you really know your parent? Time to find out!

Everyone in your family who's playing this game will write the answers to these questions for themselves. Then you'll guess how the other people playing will answer!

1. What's your favorite pizza topping?

2. If you were an animal, what animal would you be?

3. When you were little, who was your favorite superhero?

4. What's your favorite ice cream flavor?

5. What's your favorite thing to do in the summer?

6. If you could visit any place in the world, where would you go, and why?

7. What's a job you've never had that you might like to have?

8. How would your family say you behave the first thing in the morning?

9. What's your favorite room in the house, and why?

10. What's the weirdest thing you've eaten?

ART START!

Friends forever! And these friends like to wear shirts that say something. Give these friends shirts that you wouldn't mind wearing with a friend of yours!

# TAKE A HIKE!

With your parent, take a walk in your neighborhood. As you walk, take turns narrating your walk with safety tips.

You might say, "OK, watch out for that uneven sidewalk up ahead...Don't get too near the curb... Remember to look both ways before you cross the street."

You know, all the rules you've heard for years.

After you've both narrated a block or two, talk about these questions:

- Why do rules sometimes drive us crazy?
- Why do rules sometimes keep us safe?
- Does it matter *why* we keep rules, as long as we keep them? Why?
- Why do you think God gave us rules?

> Live on a houseboat? Think about how you can do this hike where *you* live.

SCRAPBOOK MEMORY MAKER!

Bestest Buddies Snapshot

Describe your child's best buddies as of this moment. Who are they? What do they and your child have in common? What do they do together? If you have a photo of your child and his or her best friend, glue it here!

3

Making Good Choices

Disciples do what Jesus wants them to do, but how can your child know what Jesus wants? Here are ways your child can be sure to make good choices.

The Point
Disciples make choices that honor and obey Jesus.

What You'll Need
- quarter
- paper
- pen
- clean paper coffee filter
- used coffee filter with old grounds in it
- two Bibles

So Many Choices
Coke or Pepsi? Plastic or paper? If only all choices were this easy!

Your child is just starting to make choices that can have life-changing consequences. Many of the choices facing younger kids are fairly black and white: obedience or disobedience, truth or dishonesty.

As kids become more independent, they deal with harder choices: which friends to hang out with, what TV shows or movies to watch, what websites to visit, and what they'll wear. And sooner or later you won't be around to help your child make good, God-pleasing decisions.

That's why you're going to provide your child with a few easy, memorable filters that will equip him to make choices that honor God and deepen faith and trust in him. Kids who start using these tools now will develop the healthy habit of thinking through decisions they face today, tomorrow, and forever.

DISCIPLER TIP

A 20-minute walk is prime time to build relationship—it's just you and your child. Talk about some of the choices he or she may be facing in school, friendships, or activities. Listen intently, and you'll discover a lot about your child!

Dive In

Heads or Tails? (20 minutes)

Before this activity, think of a place you and your child can easily walk to in about 10 minutes. It might be a local park, store, school, or landmark.

Grab a quarter, and tell your child you're heading out for a walk. If the weather is bad, take your child for a drive instead, but follow the same guidelines. Stand in front of your house and hand your child the quarter.

Say: We're going to walk to [name of the place], but we'll take a different route. Every time we come to a corner, flip the coin. If the coin turns up heads, we go right, tails, we go left. Ready? Flip the quarter, and we'll begin.

Walk for 10 minutes, following the directions "given" by the coin. You may not reach your intended destination—that's OK. Then turn around and walk back home.

As you walk home, discuss these questions:
- **How did the coin affect our trip to** [destination]**?**
- **Was this a good way to make decisions? Why or why not?**
- **What are some choices that kids your age are making?**

Say: Because you're a disciple of Jesus, your decisions should honor and obey Jesus. Let's talk some more about how to make good choices.

Dig In

Stop Sign (15 minutes)

As you near your home, find a stop sign, and stand near it with your child.

Ask: • When cars come to this sign, what are three things the driver might do?
- Are those good things to do? Why or why not?

Say: I'd be a bad driver if I stopped here, closed my eyes, and then just kept going. Drivers need to look both ways to see if any traffic is coming. They need to be aware of what's going on around them. They need to see other people around them and decide what's best to do.

In life, we all need to stop sometimes to make good choices. As a follower of Jesus, our choices should honor and obey him. Let's head home and think some more about how to make good, God-pleasing decisions.

Go inside and sit down with your child. Gather a Bible, a sheet of paper, and a pen. With your child, brainstorm (and write down) three choices your child makes on a regular basis. For example, your child might write down "what TV shows to watch," "which songs I'll listen to," and "how I treat kids at school."

Say: I'm going to give you a cool tool to use every time you need to make a choice like these. Remember the stop sign we saw? When it comes to making good choices, just STOP. S-T-O-P. Each letter reminds you of something to consider. Let's start with S.

Ask yourself, "If I do this, will I be *safe*?" Help your child look up and read aloud Psalm 139:13-14. Talk about how your child's body was created by God and is a precious gift to care for and treasure.

The next letter is T. Ask yourself, "If I do this, will I be *truthful*?" Sometimes you'll be tempted to make a choice that might lead you to lie, either now or in the future. Help your child look up and read aloud Proverbs 12:22. Briefly discuss why lying is something God hates.

The next letter is O. Ask yourself, "If I do this, will I be *obedient* to my parents?" Help your child look up and read aloud Colossians 3:20. Talk about how parents have more wisdom and experience in life than children and love their kids and want the best for them.

Finally, remember the letter P and ask yourself, "If I do this, will it be *pleasing* to God?" Guide your child in looking up and reading Ephesians 5:1. Talk about what it means to be an imitator of God—doing things that God would like.

If you answer no to any of these questions, it's probably a good idea to go in the other direction and make a better choice.

Quickly review what the letters remind us to do.

DISCIPLER TIP

As you talk about making good choices, don't be afraid to tell about a time you had to make a hard decision or a time you made a bad choice. Being honest with our kids can help them see what happens when we've turned to God—or not turned to God.

"You have brains in your head.

You have feet in your shoes.

You can steer yourself

Any direction you choose."

—From *Oh, the Places You'll Go!* by Dr. Seuss

Remember, you're giving your child a tool to use, not a test. Let your child use the examples he wrote down and practice using STOP as a decision-making guideline.

Make It Mine

Choice Filter (10 minutes)

Say: Stopping to make good choices allows you to filter out some bad stuff. Take a look at what I mean.

Show your child the used coffee filter and coffee grounds.

Ask: • How would you feel about seeing this sludgy stuff in your drink?

Say: The filter strained out all the coffee grounds. When you stop to make good, God-pleasing choices, you stop some nasty consequences from coming into your life. Bring out a clean, unused paper coffee filter. Let's use this coffee filter as a reminder that disciples make choices that honor and obey Jesus.

Choose a project from the "Choices, Choices, Choices" section (pp. 43-44) that fits your child. Or, even better, work to accomplish a project selected by your child.

Blessed to Be a Blessing

It's hard to see your children make poor choices. The consequences are painful for them and heartbreaking for you. If only you could spare them the pain.

But even in the midst of human foolishness, God does incredible things.

The Bible is packed with people who made poor decisions—David, Abram, and Martha, to name a few—but God redeemed and loved them. God still used these men and women to do wonderful, amazing things for his kingdom.

How might God work in and through your child?

We want our kids to have the tools to make good decisions, not only to help them avoid pain but also to grow closer to God in the process. As kids make it a habit to look to God, they'll grow in their faith. They'll

"I keep asking that the God of our Lord Jesus Christ, the glorious Father, may give you the Spirit of wisdom and revelation, so that you may know him better."

—Ephesians 1:17, NIV

discover what it means to hear God's voice. They'll learn to rely on God's wisdom.

- How does your child see you relying on God in the face of big decisions?
- Have you humbly admitted to making a poor choice?
- How can God use one of your poor choices to bring about glory for his kingdom?
- Think about a poor choice your child has made recently. What prompted your child's misbehavior? How can knowing, loving, and following Jesus help your child make a better choice?

Pray

Dear God, thank you for your mercy and forgiveness when we make bad choices. It must sadden you so much! Pour out godly wisdom into my child so that he'll make choices that delight and glorify you. May his first thought be to look to you for guidance. Amen.

Choices, Choices, Choices

Objective: To consider how obeying Jesus filters out some nasty consequences from our lives.

Jigsaw Puzzles

Help your child use a concordance to look up several verses about wisdom, such as Proverbs 3:5. Let your child write a few verses on the coffee filter. Your child may want to use the filter as a bookmark or simply hang it in a prominent place in his or her room.

SuperBalls

With your child, gather leaves, grass, or pebbles and drop them into a glass of water. As you add items to the water, encourage your child to talk about some of the choices he or she might be facing in the coming week, month, or year. Hold the filter over an empty glass and let your child pour the dirty water over the coffee filter.

Teddy Bears

Let your child drip dots of colored water onto the coffee filter. As the color spreads, blending with other colors, talk about how our choices influence those around us. Discuss specific family members or friends who are affected by the decisions your child makes each day.

EXTRAS!

 ## FILM FUN!

Ready for a movie? Have a parent preview the film before you watch it. Butter up the popcorn, and enjoy the movie!

Film: *Jimmy Neutron: Boy Genius* (rated G)
Length: 82 minutes

Plot

A military base sends jets to see why a blip is showing on their radar screen. Surprise—it's a boy driving a homemade rocket!

Jimmy Neutron is a young inventor. His inventions don't always work. They sometimes get Jimmy in trouble.

But when his toaster/satellite draws aliens to Earth, the aliens kidnap all parents—and Jimmy gets the chance to save the day. Maybe.

The Connection

As you and your parent watch this movie, look for how Jimmy makes choices. How does he decide what's right and wrong?

As a disciple, you need to make good choices. Jesus isn't here in person to ask—which would make things easier! So how exactly *do* you make good choices?

Like Jimmy, you make choices based on what you think is right and wrong. As a disciple, it's important you make sure that what you think is right is what *Jesus* thinks is right.

Along the way, as you grow as a disciple, you'll discover where Jesus is headed and what he's asking of you. And you'll learn to hear his voice. Those are all key discipleship skills.

What Jimmy thinks is right shows up in his choices. What you think is right shows up in your choices.

Do you make choices Jesus thinks are right?

After the Film

Talk with a parent about these questions:

- How does Jimmy decide what's right and wrong?
- Which of Jimmy's choices would you make in the same way? or make differently?
- Give Jimmy a grade for "choice making." Why did you give him the grade you did?
- What grade would you give yourself? Why?

 **GAME FUN!**

Choose Carefully

Ask a parent for a deck of playing cards. Take out two sets of cards with numbers on them—two "2" cards, two "3" cards, and so on, all the way up to two "10" cards. You'll have 18 cards altogether.

Shuffle and mix up the cards, and place them facedown on a table, arranged so each card can be picked up individually.

Then, starting with your parent, take turns turning over one card at a time. If you pick up a "3" and you think you know where another "3" card is hiding, pick up that card, too. If you're wrong, put both cards back where you found them, facedown again.

The goal is to match as many pairs as you can. Once you've matched a pair, set the pair aside. Each time you match a pair, you get another turn.

The catch: If you guess wrong three times in a row, you lose a turn. Then start counting again—three more wrong choices? You lose *another* turn.

So choose carefully!

ART START!

Every day is a new chance to make good choices! Give this guy a colorful blanket. As you draw, think about a good choice you need to make this coming week.

TAKE A HIKE!

With your parent, take a walk in your neighborhood. Bring along a watch with a second hand.

Every two minutes, switch who is leading your walk. Let your parent start. However and wherever your parent walks, you have to walk…and you have to walk the same way.

Then it's your turn. You can walk, run, or hop on one foot. It's up to you, but remember, your parent will get to lead again, too!

After taking several turns each, walk together (normally!) and talk about these questions:

- How did it feel to follow each other? Which did you like most—leading or following? Why?
- How was following the other person like following Jesus? How was it different?
- You both had to choose to follow, even if you felt silly. In what ways might following Jesus make you feel silly?
- How do disciples choose to follow Jesus? How do you choose to follow him?

Live in a jungle treehouse? Think about how you can do this hike where *you* live.

SCRAPBOOK MEMORy MAKER!

Document a Great Decision!

Jot down decisions your child has made that you applaud. Think about decisions made…

at school:

at home:

at church:

with friends:

with family:

with food and health habits:

Talking With Your Best Friend

Jesus loves talking with your child—and here's how your child can have great conversations with him.

The Point

Jesus wants you to pray—and pray specifically.

What You'll Need

- two Bibles
- several flavors of ice cream
- your child's favorite ice cream toppings, such as chocolate sauce, nuts, or fruit
- items from your pantry or refrigerator, such as pickles, salad dressing, broccoli, and fish
- bowls
- spoons
- inexpensive notebook (This will become your child's prayer journal.)
- pencil
- Prayer Pages

Specific Prayers

Most public prayers heard at the church and at dinner tables are so general that we wouldn't notice if God actually answered them.

Think about it: When you ask God to bless you, how will you know if he does? Precisely what did you have in mind?

But when you pray *specifically,* you're able to see God work—and know he's active in the lives of his people.

If your child has been raised in the church, he or she is familiar with the miracles performed on behalf of God's people. Boats floated, seas split, lepers were healed, and people were raised from the dead. Sunday after Sunday, the focus is on God constantly making himself known in spectacular ways.

So is it any surprise your child might wonder if God is still in business? After all, where are the miracles today?

When God clearly interjected himself into situations thousands of years ago, his people often responded with a deeper faith. They *knew* they were serving a living, caring God—one who saw them. They had evidence.

Your child will have that same reaction when he or she sees God answer prayer.

God *wants* us to come to him in prayer. He *wants* us to learn who he is and what our purposes are in life through prayer. He *wants* us to pay attention when he responds to our requests.

So this week you'll help your child discover the power of specific prayer. Prayer that—when answered—you'll know was answered.

This session might feel uncomfortable if you've never learned to pray specifically. That's OK—you and your child can learn together.

Get ready for a powerful week…one that will change your prayer life forever.

Dive In

Order Up! (15 minutes)

Set out bowls and spoons, a variety of flavors of ice cream, several of your child's favorite toppings, and a few non-treats such as pickles, salad dressing, broccoli, and fish. Be sure to scan your shelves for items that would be truly disgusting if paired with ice cream. Hand your child an inexpensive notebook and a pencil.

Say: I want to make you the best ice-cream sundae on the planet. Look over the selection here, and then write down exactly what you want me to put in it.

When your child has completed the recipe, send him or her to another room. Then scoop up the tasty treat, following your child's order. Scoop up a sundae for yourself; then take the treats and join your child.

Ask: • What was going through your mind while you were waiting in here?

• Did you trust me to give you what you'd asked for? Why or why not?

• How do you know that I gave you what you asked for?

• Say one word that describes how you felt when you looked into your bowl.

Say: I wanted to give you what you asked for because I like when you feel [if it's appropriate, say the word your child mentioned]. **Prayer is a little like this. Jesus wants you to pray—and *pray specifically*. Let's explore that a little more.**

Dig In

A Loving, Heavenly Father (20 minutes)

Say: Think for 15 seconds about all the things you've ever asked me for. It could have been at Christmastime, for your birthday, or anytime. After 15 seconds, continue: **Now, use your notebook to make a list of everything you can think of. You have one minute. Go!**

Time your child for one minute, and then ask your child to read the list. As he reads the list, talk about the items you gave your child.

Say: I love you, and I love giving you the things you ask for. The Bible has a passage that reminds me of that. Help your child look up and read aloud Luke 11:5-10. Ask:

Ask: • What does this passage tell you about God?

• What does this passage tell you about prayer?

Say: Let's keep reading. Have your child read Luke 11:11-13. Repeat the questions above.

Tear out the sheets of paper your child has written on, and hold up the notebook.

Say: This notebook is your very own prayer journal. Write specific prayer requests and praises in it every day. Also write about God's answers to prayers. That way you can see and remember how God answers prayer.

When God answers no, you may even be able to look back and understand why he said no.

Jesus wants us to pray—and pray specifically. But that doesn't mean he's like Santa Claus or a genie in a lamp. These guidelines will help you pray specific, God-honoring prayers.

Help your child write the following guidelines on the first Prayer Page.

- *Is this request specific?* How will I know when God answers the prayer? (Remember, God can answer prayers "yes," "no," or "not now.")
- *Is this request selfish?* Do I want God to give me something just because I like it or because it might hurt someone I don't like?
- *Does this request line up with the Bible?* Am I asking God for something he's clearly against?
- *Is this request wise?* Would it really be a good idea for this to happen or for me to receive this?

Help your child write three prayer requests or praises, practicing making the prayers specific. You may want to choose one color of ink for requests and another color for God's answers. Encourage your child to keep the prayer journal handy, where he or she can keep track of prayers on a daily basis.

Make It Mine

Specificity Practice (10 minutes)

Ask:
- Why do you think it's important to write your prayers down?
- What do you think it'll be like to read these Prayer Pages in a year? What do you think you'll discover about God?

Say: Sometimes we forget that God answers our prayers. When you look back and see what God has done, you'll see how God has answered prayer throughout your life.

Jesus wants you to pray—and pray specifically. Let's practice that right now.

Spend time praying. It may feel awkward at first, but be diligent. You're modeling prayer that will shape your child's faith for a lifetime!

Say: Now I'm going to write on a Prayer Page some specific prayers for your life. I'll add to my list of prayers in the next few weeks and then place that list in our baton. When we wrap up our discipling program, I'll take out the list and show it to you.

BATON PRAYERS

Write your prayers on Prayer Pages (photocopy page 144). Once you've finished writing, roll up the Prayer Pages and place them in the baton. You'll take them out when it's time to write again.

"Expect great things; attempt great things."
—*William Carey*

Be sure to actually do what you've promised: Ask God for specific things in your child's life. Perhaps it's a godly wife or husband, a sense of calling, or for a talent to blossom into something that effectively serves God. Be specific…and be long-winded. God wants to hear from you about your child!

Note: Before doing this activity with your child, be certain to review the baton and Prayer Page information (pp. 8-9).

Choose a project from the "Practice Praying— Specifically!" section (p. 55) that fits your child. Or, even better, work to accomplish a project selected by your child.

Blessed to Be a Blessing

We parents are probably some of the worst model pray-ers kids ever see. What parent hasn't rattled off a hurried, perfunctory prayer just to get the kids in bed or to eat dinner while it's still hot?

Not exactly great modeling.

As you know, your child is watching. So take advantage of every moment. That doesn't mean your prayers need to be long or use King James English. Keep your prayers short, sweet, and specific. And when God answers, celebrate!

- What specific things are you praying for your child?
- How has God answered your prayers for your child? How have you thanked God?
- Have you shared God's answers with your child?
- How has God answered your child's prayers?

Pray

Dear God, I want eyes that see what you're doing in and around me. I want to cooperate with your purposes. Teach me to pray specifically—and then to faithfully obey you when you make your will clear. You're a good God, no matter how you answer my prayers. Amen.

"A grandfather was walking through his yard when he heard his granddaughter repeating the alphabet in a tone of voice that sounded like a prayer. He asked her what she was doing. The little girl explained: 'I'm praying, but I can't think of exactly the right words, so I'm just saying all the letters, and God will put them together for me, because He knows what I'm thinking.' "

—*Charles B. Vaughan*

Practice Praying—Specifically!

Objective: To develop a habit of regular, specific prayer.

Jigsaw Puzzles

Help your child brainstorm specific topics he or she might reflect on during prayer time each day—for example, praying for your country, extended family members (by name), his school, or teachers. Let your child write one topic on a square of a calendar. Each day, your child can lift up specific prayers or praises about the topic for that day.

SuperBalls

Prayer doesn't have to be done with bowed head and closed eyes! Help your child come up with five attributes of God. Go for a walk around your neighborhood and look for signs of those attributes. For example, you might see a huge old tree that reminds your child that God is mighty. Help your child lift up a prayer of praise, thanking God for that specific attribute.

Teddy Bears

Help your child send an e-mail or write a letter to friends and relatives, asking how he can pray for them specifically. If your child feels comfortable, he may want to call and ask personally.

As the responses come in, direct your child to write his requests or praises on Prayer Pages. Then join with your child in praying for these specific things.

EXTRAS!

 ## FILM FUN!

Ready for a movie? Have a parent preview the film before you watch it. Butter up the popcorn, and enjoy the movie!

Film: *The Miracle Worker* (1962, unrated)
Length: 106 minutes

Plot

Helen Keller was blind, deaf, and mute. That means she couldn't see, hear, or speak. She couldn't communicate with her world.

Her family couldn't handle Helen. She was angry, frustrated, and sometimes violent.

A blind tutor named Annie Sullivan took the job of controlling Helen. But Annie wanted to do more than teach Helen to sit and eat quietly. Annie wanted to communicate with Helen…and for Helen to communicate back.

The Connection

Like Annie, God wants to do more than control you. He wants a friendship with you, and he wants to communicate with you.

This story isn't make-believe. It really happened! Annie and Helen were real people.

Look for how the friendship between Annie and Helen changes when Helen starts to "listen" to Annie and communicate in return.

After the Film

With a parent, talk about these questions:
- Describe a time you wanted to say something important but others weren't listening. How did that feel?

- Describe a time *you* weren't listening when a teacher was talking. How did *that* turn out?
- How do you feel when people don't listen to you? How do you think God feels when people don't listen to him?
- What might change if we listened to God more and told him what we're thinking and feeling?

 ## GAME FUN!

Gimme a Minute

It feels as if you can talk about anything with your best friend, right? Let's practice talking—about anything!

One at a time, ask everyone playing to talk for 60 seconds about one of the following topics, even if the person knows nothing about it!

Everyone's speech must be nonstop. No pausing to think. No changing subjects!

Some topics:
- why frogs are green
- fun things to do with parking meters
- our friend, the dime
- 10 reasons sleep is a good idea
- why schools should be open only three days each week
- why my favorite songs are the best songs in the world

Add your own topics and see if your parent(s) can talk for 60 seconds straight!

ART START!

Looks like you and Jesus are chatting, but this picture needs help. Draw Jesus and yourself. As you draw, think about what you'd like to discuss with Jesus.

 # TAKE A HIKE!

With your parent, take a walk in your neighborhood. For the first five minutes, say absolutely nothing. No talking at all.

Then discuss the following questions as you finish your walk:

- Which is more fun: talking as we walk or staying silent? Why?
- How much could we learn about each other if we never spoke?
- How much could we learn about each other if we spoke but never listened?
- In what ways do we speak to Jesus? In what ways do we listen?

Live on top of a mountain? Think about how you can do this hike where *you* live.

SCRAPBOOK MEMORY MAKER!

Prayer Penny

Hold a penny as you pray—*specifically*—for your child. Jot down what you prayed, and tape the penny here. Many years from now, it will be precious to your child (as were your prayers!).

5

Letters From a Friend

If a friend wrote your child a letter, that letter would be eagerly read. The Bible is a letter from Jesus! Here's how to help your child see the value of diving into the Bible.

The Point
Disciples must know and live Bible truth, starting with the fundamentals.

What You'll Need
- kickable ball
- trash can lid or other large, flat, solid item to use as a shield
- two Bibles
- pen
- paper
- Prayer Pages

Making the Bible Relevant
If you were doing a report on Bolivia, would you grab the encyclopedia and begin at the beginning?

No.

You don't really care about the wonderful peculiarities of aardvarks. You're not interested in the charms of an abomasum (fourth stomach chamber of a ruminant—look it up).

Unless aardvarks and abomasa are Bolivia's chief exports, they're of zero interest. You need information about Bolivia.

The same is true for introducing new believers to the Bible. They're most interested in passages that are relevant, that answer questions they're asking, and that speak to them where they are.

It's essential that new believers—including children—engage in Bible study. Otherwise, they don't benefit from the guidance the Bible provides. When they memorize key passages, they're more protected in times of temptation.

As you disciple your child, encourage her to memorize specific passages. Those specific, key "life verses" are like armor, guarding a child's heart and mind today and for years to come.

We'll suggest some life verses that address specific issues in new believers' lives. Please take seriously the need to help your child learn these verses as you learn them (yup, you'll model this!), and to not only learn the words but let their truth sink deeply into your minds and hearts.

Dive In

One-Armed Goalie (15 minutes)

Meet your child outside with a soccer ball or other kickable ball. Determine what will be your goal, and station your child in front of it. Your goal might be "that fence" or "between those trees." It needn't be anything elaborate.

Be sure the size of the goal is in proportion to your child's age and ability. For example, if your child is small, make a smaller goal so she can protect it.

Say: You're the goalie, and I'm going to take some shots at the goal. Let's see how well you can keep the ball out of the goal. Ready? Oh, wait…I almost forgot. Raise the hand that you write with. Now put that hand behind your back. You can't move it or use it at all. Ready?

Back up a bit, and take a few shots at the goal, always aiming for the side where your child is least protected—the arm that's behind her back. After a few minutes, stop and ask:

• What word best describes how that felt?

Say: It looks like you need some help on that side.

Hand your child the trash can lid. She can hold it any way she wishes and use it to help protect the goal. Play

DISCIPLER TIP

In the days and weeks leading up to this session, prayerfully consider what life issues your child wrestles with. It may be honesty, doubt, selfishness, or anger. Take the time to think and pray about your observations. You know your child pretty well, but God knows her even better!

again, continuing to aim for the weaker side. Your child should find it easier to defend the goal.

After a few minutes, take the ball and give your child a high five—and maybe a drink of cold water!

Ask: • What was the difference between the first part of the game and the second part?

• Why do you think I aimed for your right [or left] side every time?

• How did you feel when you had a shield to help you?

Say: As you grow in your friendship with God, there's someone who would like for you not to grow closer to God. That's Satan. He's God's enemy and spends a lot of his time trying to find ways to keep us from becoming better friends with God.

Just as I always shot for your weak side, Satan wants to find where you're the weakest and use those weaknesses to pull you away from God.

Fortunately, God has given you a shield: the Bible. That's why disciples must know—and live out—Bible truth, starting with the basics. So what are those basics?

Dig In

Life Issues, Life Verses (20 minutes)

Say: The Bible—God's Word—is life-changing and important. It's also huge—so big you might feel like it's too hard to find the stuff in here that's most important to you.

So first let's think about the issues or topics that are important to you. Think quietly while I read some questions. Write some of your thoughts on a sheet of paper. No one needs to see them except you.

• What are one or two areas of weakness that Satan might find in your life?

• When do you feel as if you've let God down or aren't doing what he wants you to do?

• Complete this sentence: "If I were meeting Jesus face to face, I'd hope he didn't know that I…"

Say: Now, tear up that paper and throw it away. Think about the things you wrote down. They probably mostly fall into one of these three areas of weakness:

• wanting to please yourself,
• wanting the sinful things you see, or
• being too proud of what you have (and who you are).

DISCIPLER TIP

Ideally, you should play this game outside as a way to engage a child's whole body. However, if you don't have a playing area or the weather is bad, you can play at the dining room table using a pingpong ball or even a folded paper "football."

DISCIPLER TIP

If your child isn't familiar with her Bible, take five minutes to give a "crash course" in the basics of using the Bible. Point out the books of the Bible in the table of contents, and then explain that each book has chapters and verses (large numbers and small numbers).

Say: Let's call these things life issues. (Everyone has at least one!) In the Bible, God tells us how to face our life issues.

If you had to pick just one of those three weakness areas I mentioned [repeat them], which one do you think is the hardest for you right now?

Let's look in the Bible to see what God has to say about that specific life issue.

Use the life issue verses listed at the end of this session (pp. 72-75) to guide your child in looking up and reading relevant Scriptures. Select short, easy-to-remember passages that will be meaningful and helpful to your child. You may need to look up several verses to find ones that really click with your child.

Encourage your child to write each Scripture passage on a Prayer Page. After each one, ask:

- Think of a time this passage could help you from sinning. How will knowing these verses deepen your friendship with God?

Say: I'm so glad God gives us help in the Bible! Jesus wants his disciples to know—and live out—Bible truth, starting with the basics. Now that you know some basics, let's see what it means to live them out.

Make It Mine

Memory That Matters (10 minutes)
Say: God gives you a shield. But you have to pick it up and use it! Let me show you what I mean by giving you a quick quiz:

1. What's your phone number?
2. What's your address?
3. What's your birthday?

Say: Wow! 100 percent!

Ask: • How did you know all those things?
• Why did you memorize them?

Say: We memorize things that help us all the time. That's why you need to memorize the verses you wrote down. Every day, you'll remember them—kind of like a soldier putting on armor.

Choose a project from the "Using God's Word" section (pp. 65-66) that fits your child. Or, even better, work to accomplish a project selected by your child.

Blessed to Be a Blessing

Many of us remember memorizing Scriptures to receive a gold star or piece of candy. If that's how we learned, it's likely we remember the prize more than what we memorized!

When we bribe children to memorize Scripture, we're communicating that it's a chore, that it's not important enough to do for its own sake.

Instead of offering a bribe, elevate God's Word so your child appreciates that it's a treasure—something to be held close. The Bible has the power to transform your child's heart and mind and to draw your child closer to God.

Pray about the issues that you see your child struggling with. If you find a helpful or applicable Scripture, write it on a notecard, and place it where your child will see it.

- With which life issue(s) do you see your child struggling?
- What Scriptures do you think would be most meaningful and transforming to your child?
- How can you encourage your child to continually seek guidance in the Bible?

> "The Bible is God's chart for you to steer by, to keep you from the bottom of the sea, and to show you where the harbor is, and how to reach it without running on the rocks or bars."
> —*Henry Ward Beecher*

> "The Holy Scriptures are our letters from home."
> —*St. Augustine*

Pray

Dear God, thank you for the wisdom and guidance you've given us in the Bible. I pray that you place these specific passages in my child's heart—daily. I pray that your Word will guide her through life and deepen her love for you. Amen.

Using God's Word

Objective: To learn both the words and meaning of specific Bible passages.

Jigsaw Puzzles

Allow your child to spend time reflecting on life issue passages she selected. Then direct her to write one passage in her own words on a Prayer Page.

Say: Now write three situations in which it will be helpful to remember this verse. After you write each situation, say the verse aloud. Imagine how you'll feel when you say that verse in one of those situations!

SuperBalls

Ask your child to select one life issue verse and paraphrase it. Then help your child come up with physical cues that will prompt her to say the verse each day. For example, "I'll read or recite the verse in my head every time I brush my teeth." Or "I'll read this passage when I pour my cereal each morning."

Then help your child tape notecards with the verses written on them near the place that action takes place (for example, on the bathroom mirror or on the cereal box). Rather than just slapping the notecard on the fridge, put it on the milk container or on something your child will touch or use every day.

Being specific and unique will help your child see and memorize the passages!

Teddy Bears

Commit to memorizing relevant life issue verses together. Start by saying the first half of the verse, and then ask your child to say the second half. Then switch roles. Or put the Bible words to a melody that you both know. Plan to sing the Scripture together before bedtime or on the way to school.

EXTRAS!

 ## FILM FUN!

Ready for a movie? Have a parent preview the film before you watch it. Butter up the popcorn, and enjoy the movie!

Film: *The Incredibles* (rated PG for action violence)
Length: 115 minutes

Plot

Fifteen years ago, Mr. Incredible was America's favorite superhero. But when he saved someone who didn't want to be saved, he got in trouble. He couldn't be a superhero any longer.

Neither could his wife, Elastigirl.

Mr. Incredible took a boring job until a mysterious message gave him the chance to once again pull on his super suit and head out for an adventure.

That message changed *everything*.

Mr. Incredible jumped back into his career—and that brought surprises for himself, his wife, and his children.

The Connection

How often do we get a letter (or 3-D message tablet, in Mr. Incredible's case) that changes everything?

Not often.

But there's one letter that *should* change us, and that's the Bible. It's one way God speaks to his people. And disciples need to pay close attention when God tells them something!

As you watch this movie with your parent, look for how Mr. Incredible's life changes after he gets the message. What changes are for the good, and which should he have avoided?

After the Film

With a parent, talk about these questions:

- What's a favorite message you've received from someone?
- If you wrote a letter to your best friend—and your friend wouldn't read it—what would that do to your friendship?
- If the Bible is a "letter from God," what does not reading it do to our friendship with God?
- What's the easiest thing about reading the Bible? the hardest?

 GAME FUN!

Code Talker

Keep your parent guessing! It's not hard when you give your mom or dad a note written in code!

Following is a simple code. (Well, simple if you know the secret behind it! *Not* so simple if you're trying to break the code!)

Two High Code

Write out the letters A to M. Then, right below that list, write N to Z. Your code will look like this:

A B C D E F G H I J K L M

N O P Q R S T U V W X Y Z

When you write your message, use the letter above or below the letter you *really* want to use. For example, for an A use an N instead. For a P use a C instead. Leave out all the spaces between words and punctuation. For instance, the message "I love you, Mom!" would be: VYBIRLBHZBZ

Write a short, encouraging note to your parent. Include a Bible verse you think is important for disciples to know.

Ask your parent if he or she can break the code. If not, offer hints. If necessary, show the Two High Code to your parent.

Send notes back and forth. Write to a few of your school or church friends, too! Once you understand the code, you'll write and read quickly!

ART START!

What if God sent you an e-mail? What might he say? Write what you think you might hear from God.

 TAKE A HIKE!

With your parent, take a walk in your neighborhood. Take sidewalk chalk with you. Every few blocks, write encouraging words on the sidewalk.

For example, you might write, "Have a great day!" or "Jesus loves you!"

As you walk, talk about these questions:

- How might the people who read your notes feel when they read them?
- What will our notes tell people about us, the writers?
- What does the Bible tell us about God?

Live in an arctic igloo? Think about how you can do this hike where *you* live.

SCRAPBOOK MEMORY MAKER!

A Letter From a Friend

Glue or staple a photo of your child here; then write a note for your child to discover in 10 years.

What do you want to say that's truly important?

Life Issues

First John 2:16 identifies three major life issues that lead us into sin:

- wanting to please ourselves,
- wanting the sinful things we see, and
- being too proud of what we have (and who we are).

It's likely that one of these three life issues is a common stumbling block for your child. It's not the only place your child may trip, but it's where your child stumbles most easily.

Following is a list of common sins within each life issue. Some sins are adult-oriented; we've added them to the list to help you determine your life issues as well.

Wanting to Please Ourselves

Lustful thoughts, adultery, overeating, laziness, pornography, sexual addiction and other addictions, willful disobedience.

Wanting the Sinful Things We See

Materialism, anxiety, depression, financial problems, overspending, selfishness, greed, and failure to keep commitments.

Being Too Proud of What We Have (and Who We Are)

Anger, abuse, control, gossip, bitterness, selfish ambition, road rage, racism, unbelief, spiritual blindness, skepticism, seeking the approval of others in unhealthy ways, and an unhealthy desire for fame.

Two Dangers When Reviewing These Lists With Your Child in Mind

First, you might think your child can't possibly have a life issue already. After all, your child is so young. How can there possibly be something so sinister at work in your child's life?

And second, you might look at the list and feel your stomach sink. You recognize your child in one or more areas; you wonder if somehow it's already too late, if your child is already cemented into a life of ongoing sin.

Relax.

Spiritual growth, like physical growth, is a dynamic process. And dealing with sin isn't something your child has to do alone. Remember, God's power is greater than the power of sin. And when your child does sin, God is faithful to forgive when your child repents.

This life verse activity is designed to give your child tools to address an area of weakness. Providing that training now—while your child is young—is a huge advantage for your child.

If you and your child can't decide which life issue is most relevant, do this: Have your child learn several verses to address each life issue!

Helpful Verses for a Child Who Struggles With Wanting to Please Himself/Herself

"I hope my words and thoughts please you. Lord, you are my Rock, the one who saves me" (Psalm 19:14, New Century Version).

"God blesses those whose hearts are pure, for they will see God" (Matthew 5:8).

"So now, those who are in Christ Jesus are not judged guilty" (Romans 8:1, NCV).

"So brothers and sisters, since God has shown us great mercy, I beg you to offer your lives as a living sacrifice to him. Your offering must be only for God and pleasing to him, which is the spiritual way for you to worship" (Romans 12:1, NCV).

"But clothe yourselves with the Lord Jesus Christ and forget about satisfying your sinful self" (Romans 13:14, NCV).

"The only temptation that has come to you is that which everyone has. But you can trust God, who will not permit you to be tempted more than you can stand. But when you are tempted, he will also give you a way to escape so that you will be able to stand it" (1 Corinthians 10:13, NCV).

"So put out of your life every evil thing and every kind of wrong. Then in gentleness accept God's teaching that is planted in your hearts, which can save you" (James 1:21, NCV).

"So prepare your minds for service and have self-control. All your hope should be for the gift of grace that will be yours when Jesus Christ is shown to you. Now that you are obedient children of God do not live as you did in the past. You did not understand, so you did the evil things you wanted. But be holy in all you do, just as God, the One who called you, is holy. It is written in the Scriptures: 'You must be holy, because I am holy' " (1 Peter 1:13-16, NCV).

"But if we confess our sins, he will forgive our sins, because we can trust God to do what is right. He will cleanse us from all the wrongs we have done" (1 John 1:9, NCV).

Helpful Verses for a Child Who Struggles With Wanting Sinful Things

"If you make a promise to give something to the Lord your God, do not be slow to pay it, because the Lord your God demands it from you. Do not be guilty of sin" (Deuteronomy 23:21, NCV).

"Nehemiah said, 'Go and enjoy good food and sweet drinks. Send some to people who have none, because today is a holy day to the Lord. Don't be sad, because the joy of the Lord will make you strong' " (Nehemiah 8:10, NCV).

"He has put his angels in charge of you to watch over you wherever you go" (Psalm 91:11, NCV).

"Let the peace that Christ gives control your thinking, because you were all called together in one body to have peace. Always be thankful" (Colossians 3:15, NCV).

"So humble yourselves under the mighty power of God, and at the right time he will lift you up in honor. Give all your worries and cares to God, for he cares about you" (1 Peter 5:6-7).

"Do not love this world nor the things it offers you, for when you love the world, you do not have the love of the Father in you" (1 John 2:15).

"Serving God does make us very rich, if we are satisfied with what we have. We brought nothing into the world, so we can take nothing out" (1 Timothy 6:6-7, NCV).

"God did not give us a spirit that makes us afraid but a spirit of power and love and self-control" (2 Timothy 1:7, NCV).

"The Good News shows how God makes people right with himself—that it begins and ends with faith. As the Scripture says, 'But those who are right with God will live by faith' " (Romans 1:17, NCV).

Helpful Verses for a Child Who Struggles With Pride

"God, you are my God. I search for you. I thirst for you like someone in a dry, empty land where there is no water" (Psalm 63:1, NCV).

"And this hope will never disappoint us, because God has poured out his love to fill our hearts. He gave us his love through the Holy Spirit, whom God has given to us" (Romans 5:5, NCV).

"My friends, do not try to punish others when they wrong you, but wait for God to punish them with his anger. It is written: 'I will punish those who do wrong; I will repay them,' says the Lord" (Romans 12:19, NCV).

"God has made us what we are. In Christ Jesus, God made us to do good works, which God planned in advance for us to live our lives doing" (Ephesians 2:10, NCV).

"But God gives us even more grace, as the Scripture says, 'God is against the proud, but he gives grace to the humble' " (James 4:6, NCV).

"Trust in the Lord with all your heart; do not depend on your own understanding" (Proverbs 3:5).

"We know what real love is because Jesus gave up his life for us. So we also ought to give up our lives for our brothers and sisters" (1 John 3:16).

"These are the ways of the world: wanting to please our sinful selves, wanting the sinful things we see, and being too proud of what we have. None of these come from the Father, but all of them come from the world" (1 John 2:16, NCV).

Fun, Friends, and Fellowship

We're in this disciple thing together! Here's how your child can find people to help him or her follow Jesus.

The Point
Disciples live out their faith together and encourage one another.

What You'll Need
- two Bibles
- box of toothpicks
- 4 yards of inexpensive yarn

Building Christian Friendships
So far you've been building new—and sometimes challenging—skills into your kids. Scripture memory and prayer require kids to develop a new set of "muscles."

But fellowship is natural for most kids. Kids like spending time with friends, they're pretty good at making new friends, and churches tend to provide ample opportunities for kids to make friends.

So why do we need to focus on fellowship?

While kids may think hanging out with their friends from church is a no-brainer, it's still a vital aspect of faith development, one you want your child to practice into adulthood. This session will also allow you to raise the bar when it comes to defining fellowship.

You'll help your child discover that fellowship means more than hanging out with a buddy. And there's a greater benefit than simply having someone to take the other side in a game of HORSE or a "Destructo Master Marauder" video game tournament. Show your child that Christian friendships also strengthen our friendship with Jesus.

Dive In

Pick-Up Picks (15 minutes)

Sit on the floor with your child. Take all the toothpicks from the box and hold them in your fist.

Say: We're going to play a game. We both start with five points. I'll drop these toothpicks on the floor; then we'll take turns picking them up one at a time. Sounds easy enough, right? Well, *maybe*.

If you move a toothpick other than the one you're touching, you lose a point. Let's see if either of us can finish with any points. Ready?

Hold your hand an inch or so above the floor and drop the toothpicks. Ideally, you want some to fall away from the bunch, but most of them will be touching. Play until all the toothpicks are picked up or until you're both out of points.

Ask: • Which toothpicks did you try to get first? Why?
• Why was it harder to get the toothpicks that were together?

Say: The toothpicks that were sticking near their toothpick buddies lasted a lot longer than the ones off on their own.

Ask: • Why do you think it's important for Christians to stick close to other Christians?

Say: Today we're talking about something called fellowship. That's just a word for spending time with other people. God wants his followers to hang out together, to be friends, to encourage one another, and to love one another. Let's see what the Bible says about fellowship.

Dig In

Intertwined (20 minutes)

Hold up one yard of yarn.

Say: First, let's pretend this is a Christian like you or me. In fact, we'll call this guy Christian. Christian wants to follow God and do the things that please God. Hold one end of Christian to represent Christian following God.

DISCIPLER TIP

This session is a good reminder to find places where your child can develop quality, lifelong Christian friendships. Take a look at the opportunities you're giving your child to build these critical relationships.

DISCIPLER TIP

Some kids may have trouble coming up with the names of three solid Christian friends or relatives. That's OK. Use that opportunity as a time to pray specifically for God to provide a group of close Christian friends.

Hand your child one end of the yarn.

But sometimes, Christian is tempted to do wrong things— to sin.

Hold the other end of the yarn.

Say: I'll hold this end to represent Christian's other friends. You see, some of his friends aren't Jesus-followers. They're pretty OK even though they sometimes lie, cheat now and then, and gossip on the bus ride home from school.

So sometimes Christian hangs out with them and…well, he's pulled right along with the things they do.

Pull on the string, gradually increasing the tension.

Say: He figures it's OK. I mean, lots of other people do those things, right? And all that God stuff he's learned…well, it's just for church, right?

Pull until your child loses his grip or the yarn breaks.

Ask: • Uh-oh. What happened to Christian?
• What would have helped Christian?

Say: There's a verse that talks about this. Help your child look up and read aloud Ecclesiastes 4:9-12. Ask:

Ask: • How does this verse remind you of Christian?
• What do you think this verse means?

Say: God knows we need friends who'll help us follow and obey him. That's fellowship. We're going to create a cord of three strands, just like the one in the verse you just read.

Lay a yard of yarn on the floor. Have your child look up and read aloud Proverbs 27:17.

Say: This verse talks about "sharpening" another person. An ax isn't very good if it isn't sharp. So when we talk about sharpening people, we're talking about helping them use their gifts to serve God.

This cord we just laid down will represent someone who gives you chances to use your gifts to serve God. Have your child touch the yarn and say the name of a friend or relative who encourages him to serve God.

Lay down another yard of yarn on top of the first one. Then help your child look up and read aloud 1 John 3:16.

Say: Think of someone who has given something up for you. Someone who would do anything for you…just because that person loves you. Pause.

Ask: • How does that person help you follow Jesus?

Say: Say that person's name while you touch the second cord.

Lay down another length of yarn on top of the other two. Help your child look up and read aloud Proverbs 27:6.

Ask: • Why would a friend want to wound or hurt you?

Say: This isn't about getting in a fistfight with your best friend. God wants us to have friends who don't mind telling us the truth, even if it means hurting our feelings. God knows those are friends who love you enough to help you make good choices. Think of a friend whose feelings you'd risk hurting, if it meant keeping that friend from doing something wrong. Say that person's name while you touch the third cord.

Knot the three pieces of yarn together, about four inches from each end. Hand one end to your child and stand facing each other, so the yarn is taut between you (but not too tight). Each of you should begin twisting your end of the yarn, to the right. Soon the yarn will begin to "crimp" in the middle. When it does, reach into the center of the yarn and pull the middle straight down. Bring the ends (with the knots) together. You've just made a short length of very sturdy rope!

Tie a knot in each end of the rope, and let your child pull on the rope.

Ask: • What's the difference between this rope and the first piece of yarn we used?
• How do you think Christian friends can make a difference in your friendship with Jesus?

Make It Mine

Every Body Needs a Body (10 minutes)

Say: God wants you to have close Christian friends so you can be strong when you're tempted to do wrong things. But there's another reason. Help your child look up and read aloud 1 Corinthians 12:14-20.

Ask: • How is the family of God like a body?
• What do you think God wants you to learn from this passage?

Say: We all have special gifts and abilities. When we work together—like a body—we can do amazing things for God. That's another reason God wants us to have special friendships with other Christians: so we can work together and do the work God has for us.

BATON PRAYERS

Add your prayers for your child's relationships to those prayers you've written on the Prayer Page in your baton. Once you've finished, return the Prayer Page to your baton.

Choose a project from the "Finding Friends and Fellowship" section below that fits your child. Or, even better, work to accomplish a project selected by your child.

Blessed to Be a Blessing

Be sure your child has supportive Christian relationships before he wades off into life intending to influence the world.

Find opportunities to nurture and feed your child's friendships with other Christian kids—it's like stringing a safety net under your child! Consider these questions:

- Does your child have one friend who would keep him or her accountable in a tough situation?
- If you could design the perfect friend for your child, what traits would that person have?
- What opportunities are you giving your child to develop meaningful Christian friendships?
- What sort of friend is your child to other Christian kids?

Pray

Dear God, thank you for the support and encouragement that comes when we're close to other followers. Lead my child to friends who will guide him closer to you. Help my child seek out other kids who hold your values and have a passion for you. Draw them close together and closer to you. Amen.

Finding Friends and Fellowship

Objective: To become intentional about pursuing fellowship relationships.

Jigsaw Puzzles

Help your child think and write about his gifts and abilities.

Here's an easy way: Ask your child to make a list of five things he loves to do. For each item listed, have your child write a way that might help someone else.

Ask your child to think about who else might enjoy

doing something on his list—someone who is also a Christian and willing to help others.

With that list in hand, help your child brainstorm an easily done service opportunity and invite others to participate. Meeting someone new and sharing an experience can be the start of a beautiful friendship!

SuperBalls

Cut out 1x6-inch strips of paper. On each paper, write the name of a friend or relative. Turn over each piece of paper and write a special gift or ability that person has. Let your child use the paper strips to make a paper chain to keep in a prominent place. Encourage your child to add to the paper chain as he develops new friendships.

Teddy Bears

Help your child think of three close friends—perhaps ones that were mentioned in the "Dig In" activity. Guide your child in planning a special get-together for each of these friends. Think about their likes, dislikes, and what activities might mean the most to each individual.

Remember, you don't need to spend additional dollars—most kids are happy just to spend time together, deepening their friendships.

Be sure you follow through. Give your child the opportunity to spend special time with close friends.

EXTRAS!

FILM FUN!

Ready for a movie? Have a parent preview the film before you watch it. Butter up the popcorn, and enjoy the movie!

Film: *Ice Age* (rated PG for mild peril)
Length: 81 minutes

Plot

The arriving Ice Age is a problem for animals that need to find food and someplace warm.

A woolly mammoth named Manny, a saber-toothed tiger named Diego, and a slow-thinking sloth named Sid team up instead of eating one another. They find a human baby and decide to return the child to its father. The problem is that the father is a hunter. If they take the baby to the father, he may kill them.

These natural enemies work together to live. They become friends who encourage and serve one another.

The Connection

It's one thing to have buddies—people who are friendly. It's another thing to have *friends*—people who care enough to help you even when it costs them something.

Disciples are sort of like the animals in this movie: We're up against tough challenges. We're living God's values in a world that doesn't play by God's rules. We follow Jesus when everything around us tells us to do our own thing.

We need help. God will help us find the kind of friends who will help us. And he'll help us be that kind of friend to other disciples, too.

As you watch this movie, look for when the animals go from being enemies to buddies to friends.

After the Film

Talk with parents about these questions:

- When did you see these animals act like true friends?
- What made it hard for them to be friends?
- If people talked about the sort of friend you are, what would they say? Why?
- Who are friends in your life who help you be a better disciple?

GAME FUN!

Making Friends

Let's make some animal friends!

Shadow hand puppets are an old art form—maybe because all it takes is a dark room, a light-colored wall, and a light source.

You'll need a lamp and a room that can be darkened. Remove the lampshade, and set the lamp so you can stand near the wall between the lamp and the wall. Your shadow needs to be sharp and clear on the wall.

Practice making the animals in the illustrations below. By moving your fingers slightly you can change the length of a dog's nose or the wings of a bird.

Once you've learned to "make a few friends," invite your family to join you. See if you can teach your family what you've learned. That's sort of like discipling!

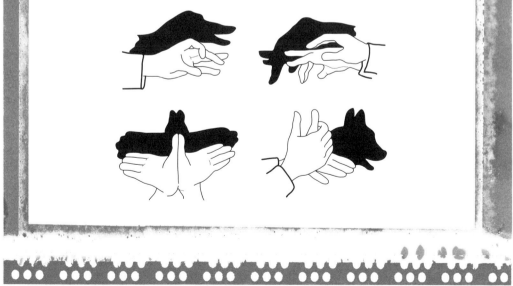

ART START!

Looks like these kids will watch a movie. What movie would be fun for your friends that would *also* help their fellowship? Draw a movie poster!

TAKE A HIKE!

With your parent, take a walk through your neighborhood. As you walk, look for the homes of your friends, your parent's friends, or family friends. When you see one of those homes, pause and offer a brief prayer of thanks for that friend.

As you hike, discuss these questions:
- What's the best thing about having friends? the most challenging?
- What's the difference between a friend and someone you just know?
- How have some of the friends we've prayed for shown us their friendship?
- In what ways has Jesus been a friend?

Live a mile from your closest neighbor? Think about how you can do this hike where *you* live.

SCRAPBOOK MEMORY MAKER!

Heroes

Your child will become like the people he or she hangs out with and admires. Who are your child's current heroes?

Sports:

Movies:

TV:

Teachers:

Politics:

Fiction:

_____ :

7

Sharing Your Story

Jesus wants you and your child to share with friends what he's doing in your life. How? By sharing your stories. You'll discover how!

The Point
Disciples share their faith stories with others.

What You'll Need
- map of your city or town
- pencils with erasers
- Prayer Pages
- two Bibles
- watch with a second hand

Everyone Has a Story
It may be hard to imagine that your child has enough life experience to *have* a story to tell. It's like seeing that an actor has published his memoirs—and he's 24 years old.

But here's the reality of God working in our lives: God brings about change. That's true in adults, and it's true in children. It's true in *your* child.

Your child's faith story simply describes that change.

A faith story includes three pieces: who Jesus is, what Jesus has done, and what that's meant in your child's life. It's that simple and that powerful.

When your child begins sharing her faith story, two things happen:

First, she identifies herself as a Christian. That's a powerful step in walking as a disciple.

And second, she begins to see opportunities to share

her story with others. God will use her to touch others. She will learn to speak on his behalf at school, at home, in friendships. Her faith will deepen as she sees God work.

Keep in mind that a faith story is a *simple* story. Encourage your child to craft and rehearse a story that's accurate—just several sentences long—and easy to present.

By the way, this is an excellent time for you to craft your *own* faith story, to share as a model for your child.

Dive In

Can You Hear Me? (20 minutes)

Say: We use telephones to talk to people far away. Imagine trying to talk to someone across the ocean without the help of a phone; you could yell as loud as possible and still not be heard.

Get out the map and set it in front of your child. Locate your home on the map.

Say: Let's try an experiment. Suppose you have some good news to share with [name of a friend who lives at least a mile away]. You've won a prize from an electronics store. You and a friend can go in and pick out whatever you can carry—games, cell phones, computers, anything. And you want to take [name of friend] with you.

Let's see if you can get your friend's attention by yelling. Yell out the good news, and tell your friend to call right away. Give it a try.

Pause after your child yells.

Say: Odd…no call from your friend. Either your good news wasn't good enough, or the message didn't get through.

Maybe you were facing the wrong direction. Consult the map. Let's figure out which way to aim your voice and try again. Ready? Yell!

Pause.

Say: Still nothing. Wow…maybe I should help. Being a parent, I have a lot of practice yelling, you know. Together let's yell, "[Friend's name], **call** [your child's name] **right away to get free, cool stuff!**"

Pause.

Say: You know, it doesn't matter how good your news is if nobody hears it.

Discuss the following questions with your child:

- What would have helped your message connect with your friend?
- How would your friend feel if you gave up now and took someone else to the electronics store for free stuff?
- When someone wants you to understand a message, what helps you receive the message clearly?

Say: Jesus does a great job giving us a message in Matthew 28. He's clear, he keeps the message simple, and he delivers it in person to his disciples—who are told to pass it along.

As Jesus' disciples now, this message is for us, too.

Let's read it.

Read Matthew 28:19-20 aloud. If your child is able, ask her to read the passage. Ask:

Ask:
- What is Jesus asking us disciples to do in this passage?
- What are three ways we might do what Jesus asks?

Say: Telling people about Jesus is like sharing good news with a friend: We have to be close enough so the friend can hear us. And we have to share the message in a way that makes sense to our friend. It helps if we're clear, too.

Let's figure out how we might share the good news about Jesus. We'll practice together so we're ready when Jesus wants us to share his good news.

Dig In

Your Faith Story (15 minutes)

Say: When we share our faith stories—the stories of what Jesus has done for us—it's important that we keep our message clear and simple. When we try to give too much information to someone, things get confusing.

Here's an example.

Suppose you asked me if I had a favorite song, and I said the following:

"Yes, I do. It's 'With a Little Help From My Friends' by the Beatles. John Lennon and Paul McCartney wrote the song, and Ringo Starr sang it on the *Sgt. Pepper's Lonely Hearts Club Band* album, which was released in the United States in June of 1967.

"The Beatles started recording the song one day in March 1967, and finished it at 7:30 the next morning at the Abbey Road Studio in London.

"The song was ranked number 304 on Rolling Stone magazine's list of the '500 Greatest Songs of All Time.' It has

BATON PRAYERS
Add your prayers for your child's ability to be faithful in reflecting Jesus' values in a culture that often doesn't. Once you've finished, return the Prayer Page to your baton.

been number one on the British singles charts three times: in 1968, 1988, and 2004."

All you wanted was a simple answer, but I flooded you with facts.

That happens when we try to tell people about Jesus, too. There's so much to tell that we try to get it all in—and people stop listening.

So let's see if we can keep our faith stories short, clear, and personal.

Our faith stories have three parts:

• who Jesus is,

• what we were like before we knew Jesus, and

• how Jesus has changed our lives.

Everything else—Moses and the Ten Commandments, Jonah in the belly of a huge fish, the parables Jesus told—can wait. They're good to know but not the most important thing to share with someone who doesn't know Jesus.

This is going to feel a bit like homework, but it's homework we'll do together. I need to sort out my faith story, too.

Both you and your child will need a Prayer Page and pencil with a substantial eraser; you'll both be writing and editing your individual faith stories.

Say: At the top of the page, write, "Jesus is..." In the center of the page, write, "Before I met Jesus, I was..." And toward the bottom of the page, write, "Because of Jesus..."

Now we'll fill in the blanks. Our goal is to be able to read our faith stories aloud in less than 30 seconds!

The first section explains who Jesus is. If a friend asked you who Jesus is, how would you answer?

Write down your child's answer; then work together to tighten and simplify the answer until it's only one or two brief sentences.

Say: Next your paper says, "Before I met Jesus, I was..." Write how you were before you knew Jesus. Maybe you were afraid of dying or of the dark. Maybe you felt guilty about some of the things you've done.

After you and your child have answered, work together to tighten and simplify your answers.

Say: Now it's time to share what Jesus has done in our lives. Let's be specific. If you were afraid of dying or of the dark, maybe you aren't afraid anymore now that you know Jesus. If you used to feel guilty about things you've done, maybe you feel forgiven now.

After you and your child have answered, work together to tighten and simplify your answers.

Next, copy your answers onto Prayer Pages, and take turns reading your faith stories to each other. Use a watch to time yourselves; the goal is to comfortably, easily share your faith stories in less than 30 seconds each.

Make It Mine

Sharing Your Story (10 minutes)

Say: This week let's enjoy the adventure of sharing our faith stories with others.

Discuss these questions with your child:

- **Who might want to hear your faith story? Who cares about you or wonders what makes you tick?**

It's tempting to choose someone who knows nothing about God, but as your child begins sharing her story, what matters is that she actually does it. It's fine to share her faith story with other Christians, too—it's an encouragement.

Begin with people who are likely to be receptive; this will build your child's confidence.

And identify someone with whom you can share your story as well.

Choose a project from the "Have I Got a Story for You" section (p. 92) that fits your child. Or, even better, work to accomplish a project selected by your child.

Blessed to Be a Blessing

There's a new "virtue" shaping contemporary culture: tolerance. This is the notion that all belief systems and opinions are equally valid and equally true.

While this belief is wonderful for avoiding conflict and encouraging political correctness, it places your child in a tough spot. It may cause her to wonder if sharing her faith story with another person is an act of intolerance.

This "virtue" stands in stark opposition to the Gospel.

Yes, it's good to be tolerant and accepting. Jesus modeled both attributes many times, but he never stepped away from proclaiming the truth, too. He could love a sinner and hate sin at the same time.

Here are some examples of faith stories to help you see how yours might look:

Jesus is God's Son, and he's my forever friend. Before I met Jesus, I felt alone. Now I know I'm loved, and I never feel lonely.

Jesus is God's Son, and he came to earth because he loves us. Before I knew Jesus, I was often sad because my parents split up. Now I know that even when things are hard in my life, I have a friend who loves me and helps me feel better.

Probe how deeply "tolerance training" has influenced your child's worldview. Does she understand that sharing her story is just that: sharing her story? That she has every right to share what Jesus has done and is doing for her? That stating a personal position isn't an imposition; it's an invitation to enter into dialogue?

Give your child permission to share her faith story by letting her see you share yours.

- What do you expect will be most challenging for your child in sharing her faith story?
- How can you encourage your child this week?
- How open are you to sharing your faith story? What obstacles might be in your way?

Pray

Dear God, I know you expect your followers to be bold in declaring their allegiance to you, that you say those who confess you will have the favor returned when you do the same for us in heaven. Give both my child and me boldness, God—and opportunity this week to go public with our faith. Amen.

Have I Got a Story for You

Objective: To share your faith story with a friend or family member.

Jigsaw Puzzles

Ask your child to carefully think through and write down her faith story, just the way she'd like to share it. Then ask her to choose a family member or friend who lives far away and send the faith story along with a cover letter explaining that it's a message she'd like to share. Every word in the right place, everything evenly spaced and aesthetically pleasing…your Jigsaw Puzzle will love it!

SuperBalls

Organize a hang-out time for your child and a friend of choice. Ask your child to find a time during the hang-out time to talk about the discipling you're doing and to share her faith story.

Your SuperBall will discover that it's OK to share a faith story while in the normal flow of a relationship, while having fun with a friend. Sharing one's faith doesn't need to be somber or formal—it happens best in the context of relationships.

Teddy Bears

Ask your child to share her faith story with a supportive family member or friend from church—someone who'll be especially receptive. Afterward, encourage a dialogue about how sharing the faith story felt and how it might go the next time. Be sure to warmly encourage your sometimes sensitive child.

Then give your Teddy Bear a hug, and pray together for other opportunities to share your faith stories as God directs.

EXTRAS!

 ## FILM FUN!

Ready for a movie? Have a parent preview the film before you watch it. Butter up the popcorn, and enjoy the movie!

Film: *What About Bob?* (rated PG for brief violence, profanity, alcohol use, and a frightening scene)
Length: 99 minutes

Plot

Bob Wiley is a patient of Dr. Marvin, a counselor. After Bob sees Dr. Marvin several times, the doctor and his family leave on vacation. Bob finds where Marvin and his family are and shows up. Marvin's family likes Bob. They can't figure out why Marvin wants to send Bob home.

The Connection

Friends usually want to know how you are—what you've been doing and how you feel. Your friends *want* to hear your story.

But what if your friends are too tired or busy to listen to you? And instead of waiting until a better time, what if you keep on talking? Your friendships won't last long.

Some of your friends want to know about your friendship with Jesus. They want to hear your story. But you need to be careful to wait to share your story until your friends are ready to listen.

As you watch this movie, look for times Bob decides to keep talking with Dr. Marvin—even though Dr. Marvin doesn't want to listen.

After the Film

Discuss these questions with a parent:

- If a friend asked you to share your faith story, what would you say?
- How can you tell when someone is ready to listen to you?
- Tell about a time you listened to a friend and it helped your friend. What happened? How do you know it helped your friend?
- Who is someone you wish would hear your faith story? Stop and pray for a chance to share your story with this person right now.

GAME FUN!

Story Slap-Down

In a group of two or more, launch a story and keep it going. When it's your turn, pick up where the person before you left off. You're allowed five seconds of silence before you pick up the story thread and move on.

Do your best to hand your partner a cliffhanger or plot twist—anything that prompts your partner to be stuck for five seconds or longer! Here's an example:

There once was a princess who had a problem. Her problem was…

That she couldn't sleep at night. She was always tired, and soon…

She was falling asleep at dinner, facedown in the mashed potatoes. Once she even fell facedown into…

Some rutabaga soup, which turned her hair…

Green. And yellow. It was sort of plaid. But she didn't care, because…

She was in love with a local barber. His name was perfect for a barber. His name was…

Got it? Here are some sample story launchers:

- The problem with Jack wasn't his tonsils after all. Instead, he had an inflamed…

- Once upon a time there was an enchanted cowboy who…

- If Jenny had known her head was about to fall off, she probably would have worn a turtleneck to keep everything connected. But as it was…

- When the elevator doors closed, Sheila realized she was the only human on the elevator. The rest of the passengers were Martians, and they looked…

- Dan had never skipped to school, but the day he started fifth grade, he gave it a try. Everyone looked, and soon someone said…

ART START!

Look—it's you! You're sharing your faith story with a friend at lunch! Draw yourself and your friend. How would you share your story with your friend?

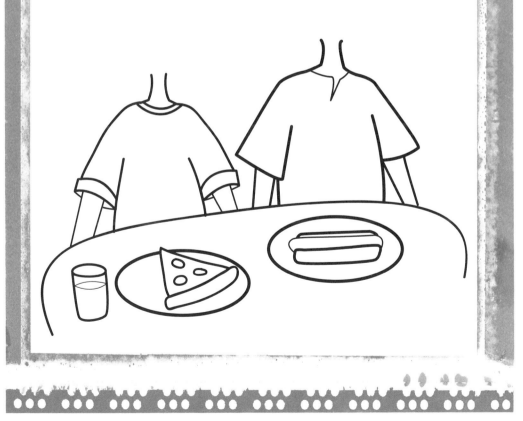

TAKE A HIKE!

With your parent, take a walk around the neighborhood. As you walk, practice sharing your faith stories with each other. Take turns with each block: first you, then your parent, then you again.

After you've shared your faith stories at least three times, discuss these questions:

- Why is it important to be ready to share your faith story?
- What's comfortable about sharing your story? uncomfortable?
- In what ways is sharing your story like taking a walk through the neighborhood?

No crosswalks in your neighborhood? Just swap sharing stories every two minutes.

SCRAPBOOK MEMORY MAKER!

Headlines

What stories are being shared in the news this week? Glue a few current headlines here.

8

Staying Strong

Disciples sometimes start out following Jesus and then wander off to follow other things. You and your child will learn how to stay strong!

The Point

Disciples grow stronger in loving Jesus and steadily better at following him.

What You'll Need

- two Bibles

Healthy and Strong

Healthy and strong.

We want those words to describe our children the moment they're born and for the rest of their lives. We want them to be healthy and strong physically, emotionally, mentally, and spiritually.

We carefully guard the health and strength of our children in practical ways—by providing healthy food and help with homework, for example. Unfortunately, some parents are less intentional about tending to the spiritual health and strength of their children. They delegate spiritual development to the Christian Education department of their churches, which is good—but there's something better.

You're better.

As your child's discipler, you're investing in the spiritual life of your child in a powerful way. God bless you for embracing your role as your child's primary faith-shaper.

Strong, healthy disciples grow in their willingness and ability to follow Jesus. Which means as your child grows in faith, he will join you on the journey of discipleship. A journey made richer by...

- spending time in prayer,
- building and growing relationships with other believers,
- spending time studying the Bible, and
- sharing your faith story.

What a privilege to walk with your child on this wonderful journey!

Dive In

Strong Arms (20 minutes)

Say: Here's a challenge for you: Hold your arms out to your sides, even with your shoulders, until I tell you to put them down.

While you hold that position, I'll tell you about someone who found himself in a similar position.

First, let me tell you how strong you look doing that. Big muscles!

Moses was leading the Israelites out of Egypt when they ran into problems. God promised to help the Israelites win in a battle with a people called the Amalekites. So God's people went out to fight.

However, God said his promise was *only* good as long as Moses held his staff over his head. If he lowered his hands, the Amalekites would start winning, and the Israelites would start losing.

How are your arms feeling, by the way? Getting tired?

Moses had to hold his arms up for a whole day! While holding a wooden staff! About now you're seeing just how hard that would be, right?

But God gave Moses two helpers—Aaron and Hur. They had Moses sit on a rock, and sitting down helped a little. They then helped a *lot* by helping Moses hold his arms up. Without the help of Aaron and Hur, Moses wouldn't have made it, and the Israelites would have lost.

Let me give *you* a little help right now. Come stand facing me, put your arms out in front of you, shoulder height, and put your arms on my shoulders.

Isn't that easier? Holding all that weight alone is really hard, but when you have someone to help keep you strong, it makes everything possible.

Go ahead and shake out your arms, and have a seat.

Pause while your child tells you how much that hurt! Then continue.

Say: What happened in Moses' life is a great example of why God wants us to be friends with other Christians—we talked about that several weeks ago. We simply aren't strong enough to make it through hard times alone.

But we *can* be strong! As disciples we can grow stronger in our faith and our ability to follow Jesus.

Read Philippians 4:12-14 aloud. If your child is able, ask your child to read the passage.

With your child, discuss these questions:
- Why do you think God didn't make us strong enough to do everything without his help?
- Describe a time you helped someone do something he or she couldn't do alone. How did that feel?
- What do you think would help you grow stronger as a disciple?

Say: We can ask others for help when we're hurting. We can pray and ask for God's help. And we can help others, too.

So let's get stronger as disciples so we're able to help more people!

Dig In

Four Limbs Are Better Than One (15 minutes)

Say: We've been practicing four habits that help disciples stay strong in our friendship with Jesus:
- spending time in prayer,
- building and growing friendships with other believers,
- reading the Bible, and
- sharing our faith stories.

But are they really important? Couldn't we just do two or three of them and still be OK?

Please get on your hands and knees. We'll do an experiment and then decide if we really need to have all four habits in our lives.

When your child is on all fours, say: **Four parts of you are on the floor right now: your right hand, your left hand, your right leg, and your left leg. If I try to push you over, it will be easy for you to stay strong and steady.**

Give your child a firm but gentle push.

Say: See? You're staying strong. But let's say we take your left hand off the ground.

Push your child again, gently but firmly.

Say: Was it as easy to stay upright? Probably not. Let's take your right hand off the ground.

Push your child again.

Say: Easier? Harder? You look a little shaky. Now let's take your left leg off the ground. How's that working for you?

Help your child up and say: **That last one really made you unstable!**

Ask: • At what point in our experiment did you start to feel less stable, less strong?

• If I offered you $100 to get in your strongest position, which of the four positions would you pick: four on the floor, three on the floor, two on the floor, or one on the floor? Why?

BATON PRAYERS

Add your prayers for your child's spiritual strength to those prayers you've written on a Prayer Page in your baton. Once you've finished, return the Prayer Page to the baton.

Say: You can forget the $100, but Jesus offers you an even better deal. Here's what James writes: "God blesses those who patiently endure testing and temptation. Afterward they will receive the crown of life that God has promised to those who love him" (James 1:12).

The four habits—prayer, fellowship, Bible study, and sharing our faith stories—help us grow in our friendship with Jesus. And what we get is a great life of adventure now and life in heaven forever!

So let's stay strong. It's worth it!

Read 1 Corinthians 15:58 aloud. If your child is able, have your child read the verse.

Discuss:

• What do you think it means to "work enthusiastically for the Lord"?

• The verse says to "be strong and immovable." What do you think might be trying to move us?

Say: My goal for you—and Jesus' goal for you—is that you grow as a disciple, that you grow stronger in loving Jesus and become ever better at following him.

Make It Mine

Daily Workout (10 minutes)

Say: This week let's practice staying strong. Every day we'll pray, read the Bible, build our friendships with other Christians, and share our faith stories with each other or other people.

Agree on a daily time to tackle the four habits together, a time that fits both your schedules. Traveling on business? Do it by phone. Need to cancel another meeting? Do it. How seriously you take this week's tasks will communicate to your child how important the four habits are.

Discuss these questions with your child:

- **Which of the four habits that keep us strong do you find hardest to do?**
- **How can I help you with that this week?**

Choose a project from the "Strength Training" section (p. 105) that fits your child. Or, even better, work to accomplish a project selected by your child.

Blessed to Be a Blessing

The wisdom of staying spiritually strong is not reserved just for your child. We all struggle to remain on the path that God has laid out for us.

The priority you place on your spiritual strength training will be reflected in the life of your child. How seriously you take the daily habits, how positive you are about diving into God's Word—these attitudes and actions speak volumes to your child.

"Sure I am of this, that you have only to endure to conquer."
—*Winston Churchill*

- What priority do you place on growing as a disciple? on staying strong? How can you help your child make it a priority, too?
- Where does your child need help standing strong?

Pray

Dear God, we parents have a weak spot—our kids. I want what's best for my child, and I know that's you. I want my child to care about a relationship with you. Please teach me to find strength, not fear, in allowing that relationship to form as you lead it. And, Lord, please use me to teach my child that you're what matters most. Amen.

Strength Training

Objective: To start the lifelong project of growing ever stronger in our faith and following where God calls us.

Jigsaw Puzzles

Help your child make a checklist for the coming week. Decide together—with your Jigsaw Puzzle taking the lead—how you'll do Bible study together, with whom you'll share your faith stories, how you'll build friendships, and when you'll pray. As you go through the week, encourage your Jigsaw Puzzle to check items off the list.

SuperBalls

Checklist? Who needs a stinkin' checklist? Your SuperBall will be delighted to discover that the four habits that help us grow in our friendships with Jesus work while we're on the move, too.

Ask your SuperBall to stay strong this week by sharing his faith story with a new friend, or by praying while riding a bike or shooting hoops or playing sports. Then talk together about how it went.

Teddy Bears

Your Teddy Bear will appreciate the habits, but it's likely that your child will appreciate time with you even more.

Don't rush through your daily time together. Approach it rested, and be patient and attentive. Ask your Teddy Bear to help identify the appropriate fellowship-building activity and to suggest a Bible story or passage to read. Keep in mind that as you disciple your Teddy Bear, not only are you drawing your child closer to Jesus but you and your child are growing closer, too.

Your Teddy Bear will love that.

> "In the confrontation between the stream and the rock, the stream always wins—not through strength but by perseverance."
> —*H. Jackson Brown Jr.*

EXTRAS!

FILM FUN!

Ready for a movie? Have a parent preview the film before you watch it. Butter up the popcorn, and enjoy the movie!

Film: *Chariots of Fire* (rated PG for brief strong language, locker room glimpse of male bottom)
Length: 123 minutes

Plot

Eric Liddell, an Olympic runner, has to make a hard choice. He believes disciples shouldn't work on Sundays—and running is work. So when Liddell's first race is scheduled on a Sunday—a race that will decide if he can run in the Olympics—Liddell must decide if he should do what he thinks is right or if he should do what everyone is telling him to do.

The Connection

Liddell believed God didn't want him to run on Sunday, and Liddell did what he thought was right. He wanted to honor God, even if it meant he couldn't run in the Olympics.

Staying strong isn't something that happens just once. Disciples have to stay strong in every decision. They have to do their best to hear Jesus' voice and to follow where Jesus leads them every day, all day.

As you watch this movie, look for moments when Liddell has to be strong. What does it cost Liddell to stick to his beliefs?

And remember, this movie isn't fiction. The events shown really happened!

After the Film

With a parent, discuss these questions:

- What are some examples of Liddell's determination to follow Jesus?
- When were you strong in following Jesus? What happened?
- What do you think helps you stay strong and grow stronger as a disciple?

 **GAME FUN!**

Let's Play Thumbthing!

It's called lots of things: Thumb War, Thumb Wrestling, even Thumb Thumping. Whatever you call it, it's time to give that thumb a workout with a contest between you and your parent!

To play, you and your parent will hook the four fingers of your right hands together. You'll clasp hands tightly so your thumbs are close together. That's all it takes—you're ready.

The goal is to pin your parent's thumb under your own without letting your parent pin your thumb. If you can keep your parent's thumb pinned for three seconds, you win.

Important Stuff to Know

- **You must start the contest at the same time**—no sneak attacks. And no using other fingers! Some thumb-wrestlers suggest starting with a chant you repeat together, so you'll know when to begin. One common chant is "One, two, three, four, I declare a thumb war." An alternative chant is "Five, six, seven, eight, if I win, can I stay up late?" That last one probably won't work, but it's worth a try. And if your parent begins laughing, it should be easy to pin his or her thumb!
- **Measure your thumbs.** Longer thumbs have an advantage. To even things up, have your parent turn his hand over so he's playing with his pinkie and you're playing with your thumb.
- **Left-handed?** The hand you use most (your dominant hand) is strongest. If you're left-handed, get your parent to use his or her left hand, too.

After you've played a few rounds, look at your thumb. Does it look stronger after that workout? No? Then you'd better keep playing!

 # ART START!

Uh-oh. This guy's strong on only one side! Draw his other half.
While you do, think about what helps you be strong in your faith.

TAKE A HIKE!

With your parent, take a walk around the neighborhood. Before you leave, decide exactly where you'll go and which streets you'll follow.

As you walk, discuss these questions:

- Some people who set off to follow Jesus wander off to do other things instead. Why do you think that happens?
- What sort of things tempt you to go off the path we've chosen?
- What sort of things do you think tempt you to wander off instead of following Jesus?
- What helps you stay faithful to following Jesus your entire life?

> Live in a lighthouse on a tiny island? Think about ways to do this hike where *you* live.

SCRAPBOOK MEMORY MAKER!

Stay Strong

Place your child's physical stats here:

Height:

Weight:

What's your child doing to get and stay physically healthy?

spiritually healthy?

9

Living the Adventure

Following Jesus is a huge adventure that lasts forever. You and your child will look ahead to what's next as Jesus' disciples.

The Point
Disciples have exciting lives as they follow Jesus.

What You'll Need
- piece of your child's favorite candy
- two Bibles
- clean cloth blindfold
- map of your country
- pencils
- Prayer Pages

A Life of Adventure
Adventure: an unusual, exciting experience. The sort of high-energy life portrayed in action movies and on television.

But our lives—waking up, going to work, spending time at church, eating pizza—is that a life of adventure?

It most certainly is.

We disciples live lives packed with excitement and adventure because we never know what God has in store for us. The Bible says Jesus came to give us a rich, abundant life, and he definitely delivers. There are abundant questions, and a life following Jesus is full of wonder, surprises, and joy. We never know when he'll send us on a mission across the street or around the world.

In short, it's a life of adventure.

Children are far more open to adventure than most adults. Childlikeness goes a long way toward finding adventure in daily life.

Not everything needs to be a thrill ride, but consider this: If you aren't experiencing some adventure in your life, are you following Jesus closely? His goal is to lead his disciples—not necessarily where we feel comfortable, but where he wants to go. If there's no longer anything unexpected in our lives, perhaps we've quit following.

Embrace discipleship. Embrace adventure.

Dive In

Listen Up (20 minutes)

Before beginning this activity, hide a piece of your child's favorite candy where it's not visible but where your child will be able to reach it. Don't give your child any clues to where the candy is lurking!

Say: I hid a piece of candy I know you like. If you can find it, it's yours. I won't tell you where it is, but I'll lead you to it.

The trick to this is that you won't be able to see where you're going.

Help your child secure the blindfold.

Say: Can you see me? No? Great, you shouldn't be able to see anything. But if you listen to my voice and do what I say, the candy will be yours in no time.

Guide your child on a roundabout path to the candy, describing any obstacles in the way. Explain how to avoid the obstacles and, when your child reaches the candy, tell her how to retrieve it from the hiding place.

Ask your child to take off the blindfold and talk with you as she enjoys the candy.

Ask: • What made it difficult to find the candy? easy?
• When did you most feel like taking off your blindfold?
• What would have changed if I had steered you into a wall?
• What about this experience made it an adventure?

Say: Notice this: You were in your own home. You were being directed by someone who loves you and who you could trust. You knew at the end of the experience you'd get your favorite candy.

DISCIPLER TIP

Look for teachable moments. If a light bulb pops on over your child's head because he grasps a new idea, stop and talk about it. The lessons learned during your discipling time need to stay with your child forever, so don't rush. If a session takes an extra 30 minutes, it's time well spent.

What made this an adventure was that you ran into some unexpected things along the way. You took some turns you may not have expected.

Being a disciple is a lot like that.

Ask: • How do you think it might be the same? different?

Say: As disciples, we know where we're going: heaven. We know whose voice to follow: Jesus'. We know pretty much what he wants us to do.

What makes life an adventure is that he often asks us to do something unexpected—to talk with someone we don't know or go somewhere new or give away something we like—or for God to care for us in ways we never expected.

Do you want to have a boring life? Neither do I! I'd rather have as much adventure as I can with God guiding me through and keeping me safe.

Ask your child to read 1 Corinthians 10:13 aloud.

Say: God promises he'll never hit us with something we can't handle with his help. He also promised to give us an abundant life. An abundant life is a life full of love and joy. Disciples get lives full of adventure, not boring lives just anyone could have!

Read Psalm 119:105 aloud. If your child is able, ask your child to read the passage.

Ask: • God's Word lights the path for our feet, but it shows only a little of the path in front of us. We can't see everything that's coming. How do you feel about that?

Say: It takes trust to follow Jesus when we're only shown a step at a time. It takes practice to hear his direction. But disciples get better at both seeing and hearing the direction Jesus sends us! Practice helps us enjoy the adventure more!

Dig In

Planes, Trains, and Automobiles (20 minutes)

Place a map of your country on a table. Find your current location on the map. Circle it.

Say: Here we are. What point on this map looks farthest away to you?

Circle the point your child chooses.

Say: Let's pretend to travel there. You're in charge of your trip, and I'm in charge of mine. We can each pick the way we want to get there, so pick the one that's the most fun or the most direct. It's up to you.

You could ride on a train. You could drive yourself. You could take a bus to New York, hop a boat to Charleston, fly a plane to Los Angeles, then swim up the coast to Monterey, and pogo stick the rest of the way. It's your call.

Jot your ideas on a Prayer Page as you think about it. You'll have three minutes to decide your route and methods of transportation.

I'll work on my notes at the same time.

Take care to come up with an unpredictable route and odd methods of transportation (riding a kangaroo? a llama?) so you and your child have wildly differing methods to reach your destination.

After three minutes have passed, compare plans.

Say: Looks like we're both going to end up at the same place, but we're taking *way* different routes to get there!

Being a disciple of Jesus is like that. Those who love and follow Jesus end up in heaven, but God gives us different adventures on the way there.

Some disciples live here in our town. Others are sent overseas to be missionaries. Some get to heaven quickly. Others serve on earth for 80 years or more.

Still, we're all going to the same place. The adventure is in the journey.

Read Matthew 4:18-20 aloud. If your child is able, have him read the passage.

Say: Peter was a fisherman. He grew up knowing he'd be a fisherman his whole life, doing what his father did for a living. Then something changed. Jesus came along. And instead of being a fisherman, Peter became a fisher *of* men—an entirely new direction, but one that let him follow Jesus.

Peter's story is like the story of the other disciples in the Bible. When Jesus said, "Here's what I want you do," all of them said, "OK."

Discuss the following questions with your child:

• If you were in Peter's sandals, would you say OK to Jesus, even though you didn't know what he had planned for you?

• Are you someone who likes surprises, or do you like everything to go according to plan?

Say: As disciples, we're on an adventure as we love, follow, and serve Jesus. We're his to direct, his to use. What a great thing!

Make It Mine

Nothing Adventured, Nothing Gained
(5 minutes)

Say: Keep an eye out for signs of adventure this week. If a new person introduces himself, ask yourself how God can use your time together. If you watch a movie, think about what God might want you to learn from it. Look for God using everyone and everything. When something unexpected happens, look for how God uses it in your life.

Sometimes life seems pretty dull. You go to school, clean your room, eat dinner, clean your room, go to bed, clean your room. But unexpected things *can* happen—and when they do, we often feel more alive, more interested in what's happening around us.

Ask: • What's something unexpected that happened to you recently? (It might have been a little thing, but you didn't see it coming.)
• What might you learn from that experience?

This week look for unexpected lessons in your own life, and share them with your child. Seeing parents take seriously the challenge of shifting perspective will make doing the same a priority for your child.

Choose a project from the "Shifting Perspective" section (pp. 116-117) that fits your child. Or, even better, work to accomplish a project selected by your child.

> "Security…does not exist in nature, nor do the children of men as a whole experience it. Avoiding danger is not safer in the long run than outright exposure. Life is either a daring adventure, or nothing."
>
> —*Helen Keller*

Blessed to Be a Blessing

Following Jesus is a huge adventure. At least, it should be.

Consider this. When you're taking your family on a trip—across town or across the country—it's usually good to plan well, to know where you'll go, how you'll get there, and what you can expect along the way. Nailing down the details is a great way to save time, save money, and avoid surprises.

But God has all the time in the world—and beyond. And money's no problem; he ultimately owns it all. And he's not much concerned about surprising us—he's calling the shots.

Like it or not, you're just along for the ride. When we're following Jesus, we need to be flexible and ready

"We can make our plans, but the Lord determines our steps."

—Proverbs 16:9

to take a sudden left turn. Our lives are truly not our own.

What God is looking to instill in your child—and you—is a burning, passionate relationship with him, a desire to love and obey him, and a high tolerance for left turns.

Look for opportunities to do some things out of the ordinary this week. There's a good chance God put them there!

Pray

Dear God, sometimes unexpected things happen, and I feel too tired to appreciate them, or the only unexpected things I notice look a lot like the wheels falling off my life. Please help me change my perspective and clearly see your hand at work. Help me view my life as you see it, and give me desire to walk through this adventure, to live this abundant life. And I pray for the same view to be part of my child's life, God. Amen.

Shifting Perspective

Objective: This week you'll practice seeing your daily lives from God's perspective: as days you're "on call" and at God's disposal at all times. Part of that process is for you and your child to stretch beyond your daily habits.

Jigsaw Puzzles

Jigsaw Puzzles tend to value routine, so even minor changes can be disruptive to them. Set the bar low; ask your child to go to school or a friend's house a different way. Ask your child to pray for people he passes while on the new route. These are people he'd have never seen had he not stepped outside his routine.

SuperBalls

No problem asking for SuperBalls to change things up; they live for adventure! Give your SuperBall the assignment to meet 10 new people this week. Point out that meeting new people won't happen if your SuperBall does the same things he usually does, goes to the same places he usually goes, or sits with the same friends he always shares lunch with at school.

Ask him to pray for opportunities to engage with new people and, after meeting and speaking with each new person, to silently pray, "God, how would you like me to serve this person?"

Teddy Bears

Some children find diving into new relationships daunting. If your child is one of them, walk through the process with him. Spend a morning or afternoon together visiting places where people tend to relax and chat with people nearby: a coffee shop, a swimming pool, a community gathering. You might even sit in a different spot at church on Sunday morning!

Ask your Teddy Bear to silently pray for each new person he or she meets, asking God, "How can I serve this person? Why have you brought this specific person into my life?"

Think Ahead

If you're attending a closing celebration next week, be sure to take your baton with you.

EXTRAS!

FILM FUN!

Ready for a movie? Have a parent preview the film before you watch it. Butter up the popcorn, and enjoy the movie!

Film: *Balto* (rated G)
Length: 78 minutes

Plot

Balto was a half-wolf, half-husky who lived in Alaska. In 1925, an outbreak of a disease called diphtheria was making children sick. Some children were dying. The only medicine that would help was 600 miles away! There were no helicopters or cars that could deliver the medicine, so a brave man led a dog sled team on the dangerous trip to get medicine and bring it back.

Balto led the team of dogs. Their journey across the Alaskan wilderness inspired other sled teams to try it. The journey inspired the Iditarod dog sled race in Alaska.

The Connection

A dog sled team and human driver take off into the wilderness. No way to call for help. No clear path. Lots of danger.

That's an adventure!

Disciples live an adventure, too. They live in a world that for the most part doesn't obey God. They have a lifesaving message to share. They are led by Jesus, who isn't scared of anything and will take them anywhere.

Disciples don't know exactly where they're going, but they know where they'll end up: heaven. They may not know what's ahead, but they know they can trust their leader, Jesus.

Want an adventure? Follow Jesus!

During this movie, look for the people (and puppies!) who are living lives of adventure.

After the Film
Discuss these questions with a parent:
- What's good about living a life of adventure? What are the costs?
- If you could have an adventure in your own town, what would it be? What would make it an adventure?

 GAME FUN!

Instant Adventures

The more people play this game, the more fun it is. So invite your whole family!

If you're playing with *just* a parent, ask your parent to decide if he or she is salt or pepper.

After your parent decides, announce that *pepper* will go first. The pepper person will have 30 seconds to think of a 30-second adventure on which to send the salt person.

A few rules:

The adventure must be doable and safe. That is, "hang from the ceiling fan while whistling" probably isn't a good idea.

The adventure must be unexpected. "Stand there and breathe" isn't an adventure. "Stand there and hold your breath for 30 seconds"— *that's* an adventure.

If someone doesn't think he or she can do an adventure, it's OK to say, "Please give me another adventure." But if you can do an adventure, do so. It's not an adventure if it's easy!

Sample Adventures
- Go to an open window and sing an opera at the top of your lungs for 30 seconds.
- Stand on one foot while your eyes are closed for 30 seconds.
- Clean as much of your room as possible in 30 seconds.
- Clean as much of *my* room as possible in 30 seconds.
- Call a random phone number and talk with the other person for 30 seconds, explaining what you're doing.

ART START!

Ever wish you could look out the window and see what's next for you? Whatever it is, Jesus will be with you. Draw what you think God might be asking you to do, and put Jesus in the picture!

TAKE A HIKE!

With your parent, take a walk *not* around your neighborhood. Instead, take a car or bus somewhere unfamiliar to you both— somewhere you've not walked before.

As you hike, look for "adventures," things you could do that you've not done before. Walk into shops or stores you've never visited. Greet people and wish them a good day. Pick up litter. Explore streets that lead to interesting places. Be adventurers!

Living in the country? Drop, stop, and snoop: Take a close look at things you pass by every day. Turn over rocks. Examine the underside of leaves. Stroll through a field or grove you usually walk past without a second glance.

As you hike, discuss these questions:

- What's fun about being open to adventure?
- How could we have an adventure in our own neighborhood? in our daily lives?
- Why is following Jesus an adventure?
- What's an adventure you'd like to have with Jesus?

SCRAPBOOK MEMORY MAKER!

The Adventure
Place a photo of your current home here:

Sketch a picture of heaven here:

What adventures might your child encounter between now and heaven?

What's an adventure your child is experiencing now at school or home?

10

Making a Memory

Deciding to become a committed disciple is a huge moment in your child's life. You and your child will make that decision one to remember.

The Point
Deciding to follow Jesus is a *very* big deal—and a decision to celebrate!

What You'll Need
(If you won't be attending a Closing Celebration as part of a church discipling program)
- the Covenant you signed in week 1
- the prayers you've written for your child on Prayer Pages
- your baton

A Special Time Together
Think about your growing-up years at home. If you're like most adults, very few days made a lasting impression. You and your parent or parents got up, did what you did all day, went to bed. The days blended together.

But that daddy-daughter dance your father took you to? The special camping trip? That time just you and your mom went out shopping for school clothes and you laughed uncontrollably when you tried on matching outfits? Those days stand out as special memory-makers, and you'll treasure them forever.

This week, create one of those memories with your child, honoring him or her for seeing the discipling program through—for making a serious commitment to Jesus, choosing to be a disciple, and then doing something about it.

Have a great time together doing something your child enjoys, something your child will talk about with friends and will remember forever.

What would make an amazing memory for your child? A night at the ballet or baseball park? A dinner out and limo ride? If so, check into making those arrangements.

Is a limo out of reach? Ask a friend with a new car to drive while you and your child sit in the back sipping sparkling cider from crystal glasses.

Would your child enjoy the time with you alone, or would he or she prefer to invite some friends along?

Whatever you do—and to be special it doesn't have to be expensive—consider how much fun you've had just spending time with your child through this discipling program.

Don't let that intimacy slip away. Plug regular times to be together into both your schedules.

Set a habit in place that will help you stay close forever!

Dive In

Par-tay!

The goal this week isn't to spend lots of money, but "having fun with child = spending money" is a common equation. That's why we cautioned you early on to set aside money for this outing.

Special outings are often special because you can't afford to do them often. "Let's go catch a ballgame" sounds great until you start adding up the price of tickets, parking, snacks, and souvenir programs.

So hopefully by now you have a budget. And you know what you want to do with your child. You've purchased any tickets you need, made whatever reservations you require, and cleared the calendar so you and your child are both available.

Or…not.

Maybe you're still not sure what to do to create a positive memory-maker, a "boy, I remember when…" moment.

If you're still scrambling, relax; there are plenty of options. And it doesn't necessarily have to cost a fortune. Remember that what will make the experience truly fun is that you're doing it together. And that at some point you make eye contact, tell your child how proud you are of him or her, and you then talk about how the past few weeks have changed you both.

A quick list of inexpensive suggestions ends this chapter (see "Ideas for Your Outing" on pages 127-128). Review them if you're still unsure what might make a memorable time together and you need a spark to ignite your own ideas.

If you won't attend a closing celebration as part of a group, this is your last discipling meeting—and the time to review, to pray for and bless your child, and to pass your baton to your child.

Review

Before you launch into your time with your child, while you and your child are alone, discuss the following questions:

- **What do you think you will remember from this discipling experience 10 years from now?**
- **If you could spend more time on any part of this discipling process, what would it be? What would you want to do?**
- **What part of the past few months challenged you? Why?**
- **In what direction do you think Jesus is taking you as you follow him?**

Pray a Blessing Over Your Child

Another special part of your time together this week is praying a blessing over your child. The practice was commonplace in biblical times, and it's just as powerful today.

This discipling process has helped you see your child in a new light. Perhaps you've marveled at how your child is growing. You've caught glimpses of how God can use your child to honor God and to touch the world.

Blessing your child is simply letting your child hear what you've discovered—and feel the deep joy of hearing how she's valued by God and by you.

Here's how to compose a biblical blessing that would do a patriarch proud:

- Compose a brief statement about who your child is in Jesus—a child of God, beloved by God, whatever you wish to emphasize.
- Add a few words about the child's character or a promise made by God to the child.
- Speak statements of hope for your child that are meaningful to you, such as a desire that your child stay faithful, remain pure, or marry a Christ-follower.
- Add a statement that summarizes your love for your child and God's loving promises to your child.

After receiving your blessing, your child will feel loved, cherished, and precious. And you'll feel the love of God flow through you into the life of your child.

If your special time includes your child's friends, pray a blessing for your child before the friends arrive. Make this an intimate, connected moment by facing your child, making eye contact, and telling your child how proud of him or her you are. And don't let your words be forgotten; write down the blessing you share, and tuck it into your baton.

Lay a hand on your child's head. If God has given you any insight into your child's unique abilities and character over the past 10 weeks, thank God for those gifts. Name them, and ask God to use them now and in the future.

Share the prayer requests you've written during the past few months with your child.

Pass the Baton

If you're part of a church discipling program and will be attending a closing celebration, you'll get a copy of the Covenant to place in your baton then. And that's when you'll pass the baton to your child. So skip this brief ceremony; you'll be doing it at the closing celebration.

But if you're going through this discipling process on your own, now is the time to be sure the Covenant you signed weeks ago is still in the baton along with the prayers you've written and a copy of the blessing you shared with your child.

Say: I want you to have this symbol of our discipling time together. It's my prayer that you'll continue to grow in your relationship with Jesus and that you'll disciple other people. The Covenant we signed doesn't have an ending date—we're disciples of Jesus forever.

I'm proud of you for the commitment you've put into the past few months. Let's continue to pray specifically, to be in fellowship, to read and live out God's Word, and to share our faith stories. Those are habits that will draw us closer to Jesus throughout our lives.

Pray Together

Together, thank Jesus for his powerful example, for his love, for calling you to be his followers. Pledge to him your hearts now and forever.

Ideas for Your Outing

- **Take a nature walk** at the local park or beach. Bring along bread to feed those birds that decide "you owe it to them."
- **Visit a bonsai specialty store** and learn how to trim a bonsai. Buy a plant, and, using it as your centerpiece at a restaurant, talk about how God is shaping and trimming both of you.
- **Go bowling,** but make it special by using only your less dominant hand. Righties bowl leftie; lefties bowl rightie. See if you can break 25.
- **Spend the evening at an amusement park.** Go on whatever rides your child chooses.
- **Take a few laps at a go-kart track.** Look ahead to your child's driving years with trepidation.
- **Window-shop in an exclusive shopping area.** Try things on. Decide how you'd accessorize if budget were no problem—and then let your child pick out something special (up to your preset amount).
- **Visit the zoo.** See if there's an event at the zoo, like an art show or musical performance. Don't feed the animals. Do feed your child.
- **Go to a local festival or specialty show.** Monster truck rally, anyone?
- **A movie,** but not just any movie. Go to an IMAX movie!

- **Arrange for a hot air balloon ride.** You won't know exactly where you'll land, but you'll have a great time getting there!
- **Line up a quick trip in a private plane** so you can see where you live from the sky.
- **Attend a concert.** Choose something you both enjoy— it won't be any fun for your child if you sit through the entire show with your hands over your ears screaming, "Turn it down!"
- **Kick back at a rodeo.**
- **Play a round of miniature golf**…with the putters turned upside down.

SCRAPBOOK MEMORY MAKER!

Memories, Memories
Glue a picture of you and your child on your special outing here.

Write five words that describe how you're feeling about your child:

11

For Groups:
Optional Launch Party

If a group is doing this program together, start with a fun event that sets the vision and builds support. Here's how to do it.

What You'll Need
- chairs
- CD player or sound system to play music
- name tags
- batons—one per adult
- Bible
- copy of the Covenant (p. 137) for each guest, plus an extra copy
- copy of *Passing the Baton* for each adult guest
- red inkpad
- black or blue pens
- party food, such as cupcakes, punch, cake, ice cream and toppings

Why It's a Good Idea to Do This With Others

It's one thing to *start* a project but quite another to *finish* it.

This discipling program is one ball you don't want dropped, so do this: Build in accountability and encouragement. Good intentions alone won't get a child discipled.

Most parents have *great* intentions, but they also have calendars packed with kids' programs that were launched but never completed—Cub Scouts who never became Eagle Scouts, musical careers that petered out before the first piccolo was paid for, tutus that ended up in the Goodwill pile.

Parents *need* the support and accountability that comes with going through this program in a group. So if there's any way possible to find a few like-minded moms and dads with whom to partner, do so.

Here's How It Works

Assuming you're in a church setting, host a launch party for parents and children who want to do this program. It doesn't matter if there are two sets of parents and kids or twenty—the support is worth the effort.

Then, as parents disciple their children, encourage them to tap into the network of other parents for support and accountability. Encourage them to pray for one another.

Get back together for a closing celebration in week 11. It's that easy.

If you're a church leader, call parents every few weeks to see how the discipling is going. There's great power in accountability, in the ceremonies used in this launch party, and in the closing celebration.

Besides, it's more fun when parents are on a team!

Get Ready...Get Set...

What fun is a party with no guests?

Long before your launch party, advertise the discipling program so parents know it's available. Describe the program through your church communications. Spread the word personally.

If you're doing a launch party, it's likely the discipling program is part of your church's children's or family ministry. With that in mind, the following instructions are intended for whoever is hosting the party.

And Go!

Select a room for your meeting that's about full when the expected number of people are in it. It's discouraging to have a small circle of chairs in the corner of a gymnasium; it looks like nobody came!

> If you're a children's ministry leader organizing this program, recruit someone to pray for each family going through the program. Ask your prayer people to check in with their families every two weeks to ask for specific prayer requests.

Place chairs in a circle—just the number you think you'll need. Have extras handy; if more people come, you can quickly enlarge the circle.

Play upbeat instrumental music as guests arrive. This is a party, after all! Just make sure that the music doesn't overpower the possibility of discussion and that your musical choice is something most people enjoy.

As guests arrive, ask everyone to fill out a name tag.

Ask each guest to write on the tag his or her first and last name and—in the upper left-hand corner—one place in his or her life the guest got lost. It may have been on a trip or while finding a classroom in a new school—anywhere it happened is fine.

When it's time to begin, slowly turn down the music and ask guests to sit down and to each make a mental note of the person directly across the circle from him or her. That person will be a partner for the next exercise. If there's an uneven number of people, jump in to be a partner.

Story Time! (15 minutes)

Ask guests to briefly share with their partners the "lost" stories hinted at on their name tags. Each partner should talk for up to 60 seconds. And it's important that partners listen carefully—guests will tell their partners' stories to a larger group!

If you have more than eight people at your launch party, have pairs join up with other pairs to form foursomes and tell their partners' stories there. That way everyone can talk, and it won't take a half-hour to get through the stories.

If you have eight or fewer guests, give each guest 45 seconds to tell his or her partner's story of woe about being lost. What happened? How did it end? Is the partner still lost somewhere on the highway or in the wilderness?

Voiceprint (up to 25 minutes)

Ask children to stand in the circle.

Say: I'd like each parent to stand behind his or her child. Children, please close your eyes—and keep them closed. Parents, in a moment I'll ask you to take hold of your child's shoulders and spin your child in a circle several times. Your child should feel a bit dizzy and disoriented about which way he or she is facing, but don't let anyone take a nose dive to the floor. Ready? Go.

While parents are spinning their children, remove a chair from the circle and stand away from the "hole" in your circle of chairs.

Say: Parents, once you're certain your child is steady, step away from your child and join me outside the circle. Kids, keep your eyes closed.

After parents exit, have them wait silently with you.

Say: Kids, keep your eyes closed. In a moment I'm going to ask one of the parents to ask you to come toward his or her voice. Only come if you know it's *your* parent. Everyone else will stay still.

Parents, when you call your children, don't use your kids' names. Just keep talking so your child knows where you are and can move toward you.

Kids, you may bump and thump against someone else while you're coming, so walk slowly with your arms out in front of you. When you reach your parent, you'll be greeted with a hug.

Here's the first parent.

Signal for a parent to stand in the "hole" and begin speaking.

After each parent has had a turn and collected his or her child, have guests silently return to the circle and move their chairs so parents are facing their own children.

Ask your teams of parents and kids to discuss:

- Children, how did it feel to make your way to your parents?
- Parents, how did it feel to be guiding your children? to see that your children were blindly moving where they could trip and fall?
- What made it difficult or easy to recognize the voice of a parent?

Read aloud John 10:1-5, 11-15. The New Living Translation version is printed below for your convenience.

"I tell you the truth, anyone who sneaks over the wall of a sheepfold, rather than going through the gate, must surely be a thief and a robber! But the one who enters through the gate is the shepherd of the sheep. The gatekeeper opens the gate for him, and the sheep recognize his voice and come to him. He calls his own sheep by name and leads them out. After he has gathered his own flock, he walks ahead of them, and they follow him because they know his voice. They won't follow a stranger; they will run from him because they don't know his voice…

"I am the good shepherd. The good shepherd sacrifices his life for the sheep. A hired hand will run when he sees a wolf coming. He will abandon the sheep because they don't belong to him and he isn't their shepherd. And so the wolf attacks them and scatters the flock. The hired hand runs away because he's working only for the money and doesn't really care about the sheep.

"I am the good shepherd; I know my own sheep, and they know me, just as my Father knows me and I know the Father. So I sacrifice my life for the sheep."

Say: What Jesus described is like what just happened with us.

You kids were in a sheepfold, an enclosure with just one opening. And you only came out when you heard a familiar voice, the voice of someone who loves you. Nobody had to tell you whose voice to follow. You knew the voice of your parent.

During the next few months, we'll learn to recognize Jesus' voice, too, to know how to follow him closely. That's what disciples do: They follow Jesus and let him slowly change how they think, feel, and act.

Parents, as you lead weekly sessions, you'll become better disciples along with your children. All of us can grow in following Jesus. None of us is perfect.

This will be an adventure for everyone!

Passing the Baton (20 minutes)

Say: You'll launch your first session this coming week. You parents are responsible for picking a time that you and your child have 45 minutes of focused, relaxed time together. It may be hard to find, but it's important!

There will be some work to do together—activities to do, discussions to have, some verses to learn. All of it is important, so please don't skip anything.

Your next step is to decide if this is what you really want to do, if you're serious about becoming a more faithful follower of Jesus. It's a big decision.

I hope you've talked about it before this meeting, but if not, now is your chance.

I'm going to ask you all to sign a Covenant of Discipleship.

Hand out a copy of the Covenant to each family unit. Place another copy next to you, lying next to an open Bible.

Say: This Covenant says what you'll do in the coming weeks. Listen carefully and follow along as I read the Covenant to you.

Read aloud the Covenant. Don't read the verses in parentheses.

When you've finished, ask parents and children to again sit facing each other. Give them several minutes to discuss:

- How will going through this together be a good thing in our lives?
- What might get in the way of our doing this? How can we get past those things?

Say: If you'd like to launch into this discipleship adventure together, please come up and sign your names on this Covenant. And when you've finished signing, place your thumb on the red inkpad and put your thumbprint over your name.

If you've decided not to do this discipleship adventure at this time, please stay seated.

After everyone who wants to covenant together has done so, hold up a *Passing the Baton* book and a silver baton.

Say: This book is for each adult. It contains the sessions you'll lead in the coming weeks. You'll also get one of these: a baton. Please keep your baton someplace your family will see it often—on the kitchen table, on the television set, or by the computer.

At track events there's often a relay race that uses a baton. One runner dashes around the track and then hands the baton to the next runner, who also does a lap. Each time the baton is passed along, it's up to that new runner to carry it.

We've all received a baton. Jesus sent his disciples out into the world to share the good news of his life, death, and resurrection. That good news was passed from one person to another, to another, to another...and now here we are. It's been passed to us.

Each of you adults will now receive a book and a baton. Your job, over the next few months, is to go through this process with your child. You'll pass the baton.

Along the way you'll learn things, too, because you're still growing as a disciple. We're all in the race—and we all have things to learn.

Pass a book and baton to each adult.

Say: Remember, keep this baton where you'll see it daily. Let it be a reminder of the important work you're doing as you disciple your child.

Closing Prayer (2 minutes)

Make this a prayer of dedication, asking God to bless each discipling relationship as it unfolds.

Party Snacks!

It ain't a party until the cookies, cake, or ice cream hit the table. Bring out munchies and party foods, and encourage guests to chat and celebrate what God will be doing in and through them.

Covenant

I want to grow as a disciple, so to the best of my ability, I will…

Develop loving obedience (Matthew 28:19-20)

Invite other believers into friendships (Hebrews 10:24-25)

Study the Bible (2 Timothy 3:16-17)

Consistently make good choices (Ephesians 4:1)

Impact others with my faith story (Colossians 4:5-6)

Pray regularly—and specifically (Matthew 7:7)

Learn to stay strong (Ephesians 6:10)

Experience the adventure of following Jesus—forever! (Galatians 5:25)

For Groups:
Optional Celebration
Party

You made it! This closing celebration party wraps up your group's discipling adventure. It's icing on the cake—and that sounds like a party!

The Point
Deciding to follow Jesus is a *very* big deal—and a decision to celebrate!

What You'll Need:
- chairs
- CD player or sound system to play music
- name tags
- batons—one per adult and several "loaners" (ask parents to bring the batons they've used to collect Prayer Pages)
- one color copy of the Covenant each participant signed for each guest
- ice cream sundae supplies: several flavors of ice cream; whipped cream; bananas; toppings such as coconut, nuts, chocolate sauce, caramel sauce; and so on

Well Done...It's Time to Celebrate!
Congratulations! You've just helped parents in your church do something God wants them to do: Guide their children into a deeper, lasting relationship with Jesus. And that's something worth celebrating!

This wrap-up party is a way of drawing the formal discipling program to a close for the parents and children who were involved. But don't worry—what's begun during these past few months will continue. Parents and children have communicated about their faith. Discussions have happened in the home. Children have come to see their parents in a new light: as a spiritual resource.

Good stuff!

And more good stuff happens at this party, so don't skip it.

Parents will literally "pass the baton" to their children, providing a powerful symbol that children can continue growing in Christ *on their own*. That simple act speaks volumes to children about God.

It's also a time to hear how your program did—what stories will become family lore and how you might like to tweak the timing or pace of your program in the future.

And—with an eye to the future—this is a perfect time to recruit participants to help you recruit additional families to participate in your *Passing the Baton* discipling program.

Nothing speaks louder than someone giving witness to the impact of this program. If you have several families whose stories are particularly powerful, make note and then ask for their help when you're recruiting more families.

Even better, invite families that are considering participating in the program to come along to this celebration to see what happens.

So…ready to party?

We thought so!

Get Ready…Get Set…

Long before this celebration party, remind your discipling parent/child pairs that it's coming, that there will be special moments in the party they won't want to miss.

Here's how to host your closing celebration!

And Go!

Like your launch party, select a room for your meeting that's about full when the expected number of people are in it.

Place chairs in a circle—just the number you think you need.

Have extras handy; if more people come, you can always quickly enlarge the circle.

Play some upbeat instrumental music as guests arrive. Select music that most people enjoy. No polka just because *you're* a fan!

As guests arrive, ask everyone to fill out a name tag.

Ask each guest to write on the tag his or her first and last name, and—in the upper left-hand corner—his or her favorite ice cream flavor, the more specific, the better. For example, Rocky Road, chocolate with almonds, vanilla bean, and so on.

Encourage parents and kids to share stories about their week 10 evenings. Both adults and kids will enjoy telling about the fun they had!

Ice Cream Convincing (15 minutes)

When it's time to begin, slowly turn down the music, and ask guests to stand and find someone who shares a taste for a different ice cream flavor. When they've connected, have them pause while you give instructions.

Say: Take 30 seconds to decide which person in your pair has a birthday closest to the third Sunday in July. That's National Ice Cream Day in America.

Pause to let pairs figure it out.

Say: If you had the birthday closest to National Ice Cream Day, you'll now have 60 seconds to convince your partner that your flavor of ice cream is better than the flavor the other person wrote on his or her name tag. Your goal is to win over your partner to your way of thinking.

Ready to try? Go.

After 60 seconds, have partners switch roles and do the activity again.

When time is up, have guests return to their seats and turn their chairs so they can talk with their discipling partner.

Ask partners to discuss:
- • How did the other person try to convince you to change your loyalty to your favorite flavor?
- • How well did the other person's arguments work?
- • Did you change your mind? Why or why not?

Allow time for discussion, and then draw attention back to yourself.

Say: What you just experienced is a lot like what happens in the world regarding our faith. As a disciple of Jesus, you can expect lots of people to try to change your mind—to change your loyalty to Jesus.

You may be told that believing in Jesus is silly, that it's for babies, that you're not open-minded unless you also try following someone or something other than Jesus.

But here's something that nobody can argue: *your experience.*

If you've learned to hear Jesus' voice and felt his love, nobody can argue that. It's *real.* It's *your experience.* You can stand firm in your loving relationship with Jesus, no matter what.

Your faith story is just that: *your* faith story. You can share it with the confidence that comes from knowing it's true.

Talk About It (20 minutes)

Ask parents to hold the batons they brought with them. And here's a hint: Just in case a parent forgets to bring a baton, have several "loaners" on hand.

Say: A few months ago, you were given your baton as a reminder that, by discipling your child, you're passing along something special to your child. You were helping your child know, love, and follow Jesus, to hear Jesus' voice and obey it.

Here's what I expect *really* happened: As you worked through the discipling, you *both* received something. You both grew in your faith. You both grew in your love for Jesus. You both enjoyed having more time than usual together.

I'd like you two to talk about what happened during this discipling process.

For the next 15 minutes, relax and discuss:
- • What do you think you'll remember from this discipling experience 10 years from now?
- • If you could spend more time on any part of this discipling process, what would it be? What would you want to do?
- • What part of the past few months felt challenging to you? Why?

Put the questions on a PowerPoint slide and project it, or make copies of the questions so discipling pairs don't have to write them down.

• What direction do you think Jesus is taking you as you follow him?

Passing the Baton...Again (15 minutes)

Draw attention to yourself.

Say: I've made copies of the Covenants we signed when we met the first time. I'd like the disciplers to come pick up their Covenants and then go back to their seats.

Distribute the copies. When everyone is seated, ask each parent and child to hold different ends of their Covenant and then bow their heads in prayer.

Pray: **Dear God, thank you for the past weeks of discipling. We know we're not done, that following you is a lifelong process. Right here, right now, we commit ourselves to listening for your voice and going where you lead. To the best of our abilities, we will be your followers all our days. Amen.**

Ask adults to roll up their Covenants and place them in their batons.

Then ask each child and adult pair to hold their baton—the adult holding one end and the child the other. Instruct them to not let go until you say to do so.

Say: Now, disciplers, please pray for the child you discipled. Pray *specifically*, asking God for what you believe your child will need in order to be a faithful follower of Jesus.

I'll close for us.

When most adults have finished praying, pray:

Dear God, you alone know the future. You know what the children here need to become ever stronger followers of your Son, Jesus. You are good, God, and we know you love these children even more than we do. Make them yours forever, God. Give them the challenges that will shape them and bring compassion into their lives. Give them the direction that will keep them ever following your Son. These disciples are yours, God. Amen.

Say: Adults, please release your end of the baton.

The baton you hold now belongs to you, kids. It has been passed to you and is yours to keep all your life as a reminder that you're a follower of Jesus, that you're a disciple, and that you, too, can disciple another person to love Jesus.

Those of you who were discipled, please pray for the person who discipled you. Pray for that person specifically. Thank God for that person pouring his or her life into yours, for his or her

willingness to be an example of a person who tries to hear Jesus and follow Jesus. I'll close for us.

When most children have finished praying, pray:

Dear God, you show us your love in so many ways. But the way that touches us most deeply is through the love of someone who is willing to share his or her life with us.

Thank you for the parents who have discipled their children. Thank you for working in and through them. Thank you that you'll continue to work in and through them as they grow in faithfully following you. Amen.

Ice Cream Sundaes (until kids are ready to leave!)

Say: We don't have all of your favorite flavors, but hopefully what we have will be OK. We have some great ice cream!

I'll bring out the ice cream and toppings. Everyone, please hang out awhile and enjoy talking with each other—and building your favorite ice cream sundae!

Date:

Prayer Page